Clyde H. Stagner

TUCSON WATER

ISBN: 978-1-4251-8829-0

*We at Trafford believe that it is the responsibility of us all, as both individuals
and corporations, to make choices that are environmentally and socially sound.
You, in turn, are supporting this responsible conduct each time you purchase a
Trafford book, or make use of our publishing services. To find out how you are
helping, please visit www.trafford.com/responsiblepublishing.html*

*Our mission is to efficiently provide the world's finest, most comprehensive
book publishing service, enabling every author to experience success.
To find out how to publish your book, your way, and have it available
worldwide, visit us online at www.trafford.com/10510*

www.trafford.com

North America & international
toll-free: 1 888 232 4444 (USA & Canada)
phone: 250 383 6864 ♦ fax: 250 383 6804
email: info@trafford.com

The United Kingdom & Europe
phone: +44 (0)1865 487 395 ♦ local rate: 0845 230 9601
facsimile: +44 (0)1865 481 507 ♦ email: info.uk@trafford.com

10 9 8 7 6 5 4 3 2 1

FOR CITIZENS OF TUCSON WHO CANNOT AFFORD BOTTLED WATER

PREFACE

Surface water shall be free from pollutants in amounts or combinations that cause odd taste or odor in drinking water (Ref: Arizona Administrative Code R 18-11-108 A).

The US EPA has designated, for potable drinking water, a Secondary Maximum Level standard for total dissolved solids (TDS) which is 500 milligrams per liter.

US EPA states that "watershed-plans should address not only the sources of water quality impairment, but also any pollutants and sources of pollutants that need to be addressed to assure the long-term health of the watershed, including both surface and groundwater that serve as sources of drinking water (Ref: Federal Register, Volume 68, Number 205, October 23, 2003)".

CONTENTS

CHAPTER 1

TUCSON WATER INTERFACES

The United States Geological Survey (USGS) is an unbiased, multidisciplinary science organization focusing on biology, geology, geospatial information, and water. The USGS accomplishes timely, relevant, and impartial study of the landscape, our natural resources, and its natural hazards which threaten citizens. Their responsive support to citizens`s requests for monitoring data and scientific studies is helpful, immediate, responsive, and supportive.

The United States Environmental Agency (USEPA) leads the nation`s environmental science, research, education, and assessment effort with the mission to protect human health and the environment. The USEPA has the responsibility of designating harmful contaminants, establishing allowable concentrations, designating measurement protocol, and enforcement of legally established concentration quantities- permittee monitoring violations are posted on the internet.

The Arizona Department of Environmental Quality (AZDEQ) is responsible for the enforcement of applicable state and federal rules and regulations applicable to potable, used water from potable sources, and sludge/biosolids disposal.

The Arizona Department of Water Resources (ADWR) works to secure a long term dependable water supply for Arizona`s communities. ADWR issues permits, which include water quality and quantity specifications, to the Central Arizona Water Conservation District (CAWCD) for the recharge of the Central Arizona Project (CAP) lower Colorado River surface water. The ADWR has five Active Management Areas (AMA) in Arizona-one of which is the Tucson AMA with headquarters in Tucson. The TAMA budgets water for nine entities in its area.

The Central Arizona Water Conservation District (CAWCD) is responsible for the delivery of lower Colorado River surface water via the CAP canal to communities in central Arizona which include Phoenix and Tucson. CAWCD operates, under permit, the facilities for recharge of CAP water.

The Central Arizona Groundwater Replenishment District (CAWRD) is a division of CAWCD for entities wanting and needing an Assured Water Supply.

The Tucson Water Department (TWD) is responsible for the quality and quantity of potable water distributed to residential, commercial, industrial, and governmental users in the potable water service area of Tucson and areas extending into Pima County located outside the corporate limits of Tucson. TWD is also responsible for distributing 90 % of the treated and treated recharged waste water effluent produced in Pima County`s Regional Wastewater Reclamation Department (PCRWRD).

PCRWRD is responsible for the collection and treatment of sewage from most of Tucson and areas of Pima County (some residences use septic tanks). PCRWRD is also responsible for the quantity, quality, and disposition of biosolids, sludge, and treated effluent to include the distribution of 10 % of the treated wastewater effluent produced.

The Pima County Department of Environmental Quality is responsible for enforcing applicable rules and regulations pertaining to septic tank use.

The Arizona Water Institute is a consortium of three Arizona Universities focused on water sustainability through research, technical assistance, education, and technology plus water management protocol. The Director`s Adaptive Management protocol is particularly applicable to Tucson and Pima County.

The Water Resources Research Center, University of Arizona, issues water explanatory articles, conducts water explanatory presentations, issues water opinions without experimentation-all with political acumen.

The Pima Associations of Government (PAG) works closely with the PCRWRD.

Stakeholders are defined by the USEPA as any organization, governmental entity, or individual that has a stake in, or may be impacted by a given approach to environmental pollution prevention, energy conservation, etc. Politicians sometimes appoint supportive individuals to stakeholder committees to assure supportive findings for political objectives

Pima County Supervisors are elected individuals collectively, and individually, responsible for the health and welfare of Pima County citizens residing in Pima County outside city corporate limits and some services applicable to Pima County and unincorporated cities such as sewage collection, treatment, and disposition; septic tank use, social health concerns, and homeland security representation.

Tucson City Councilpersons are elected individuals collectively, and individually, responsible for the health and welfare of Tucson residents.

From:	"Cheryl K Partin" <ckpartin@usgs.gov>
To:	<cstamping@dakotacom.net>
Cc:	<archive_ask@usgs.gov>; <gs-w-az_NWISWeb_Data_Inquiries@usgs.gov>; <h2oteam@usgs.gov>
Sent:	Thursday, December 06, 2007 5:32 PM
Attach:	stagner.xls
Subject:	Re: Re URL: http://waterdata.usgs.gov/nwis/annual

Hi Clyde,

I checked our database, and there are two sites on the Colorado River that are near or upstream from the entry point to the CAP canal that have radionuclide data. The sites are:

USGS 09424000   COLORADO RIVER NR TOPOCK, AZ.
USGS 09423000   COLORADO RIVER BELOW DAVIS DAM, AZ-NV

There are no recent data; the samples are from 1981 and 1986. Attached is an Excel file with the data.

I don't know if it would be helpful to you, but there is also a discussion of water quality in the CAP canal at:

http://www.cap-az.com/static/index.cfm?contentID=38

Hope this helps!

Thanks,
  Cheryl

~~~~~~~~~~~~~~~~~~~~~~~~
Cheryl Partin
AZ QW Database Administrator
ckpartin@usgs.gov
(480) 736-1093 x237

~~~~~~~~~~~~~~~~~~~~~~~~

Carole J Marlow/RGIO/USGS/DOI

11/30/07 12:23 PM

To gs-w-az_NWISWeb_Data_Inquiries@usgs.gov, cstamping@dakotacon.net

cc archive_ask@usgs.gov, h2oteam@usgs.gov

Subject Re: Re URL: http://waterdata.usgs.gov/nwis/annual.ink

CHAPTER 2

MONITORING:WATER QUALITY

USEPA defines monitoring as periodic or continuous surveillance or testing the level of compliance with statutory requirements and/or pollutant levels in various media or in humans, plants, and animals. USEPA defines pollutant as generally, the presence of a substance in the environment that because of its chemical composition or quantity prevents the functioning of natural processes and produces undesirable environmental and health effects. Under the Clean Water Act, for example, the term has been defined as the man-made or man induced alteration of the physical, biological, chemical, and radiological integrity of water and other media.

Early monitoring of hurricane parameters enables action to minimize adverse effects. Such is the case with pollutants. USEPA and AZDEQ do not limit the monitoring of pollutants by the Tucson Water Department which has not conducted some of the necessary potable water monitoring required by USEPA whereas 76 % of the permitted potable water suppliers in the United States have met the USEPA monitoring requirements. Failure to monitor as required reduces public confidence in the potable water supplier who could purposely lose monitoring samples with excessive pollutant levels. No known punitive action has been taken against the Tucson Water Department by AZDEQ.

The Tucson Water Department has not published its USEPA monitoring violations in its annual USEPA required CCR (consumer confidence report) for the citizens of Tucson. Failure to do so reduces confidence in the monitoring data cited in the CCR.

Monitoring data, if it can be obtained from AZDEQ, is given under censorship criteria. Monitoring data from the Pima County Wastewater Reclamation Department can be viewed by request. Monitoring data from the CAWCD recharge facility for input CAP surface water and Avra Valley groundwater can be viewed in Tucson AMA`s office on West Congress St. in Tucson. Results of a 2006 CAP water quality monitoring data has been published on the internet. Publishing potable water monitoring data on the internet for public access enhances higher reliability in the data compared to person to person transfer by email or in-house.

From: "cstampingr@dakotacom.net" <cstamping@dakotacom.net>
To: <mcweb@tucsonaz.gov>
Sent: Wednesday, July 16, 2008 8:48 AM
Subject: Gray water effects on private property

Dear Honorable Mayor and Council Members,

On 15 July 2008, a copy of a letter,subject as above addressed to the Tucson Pima Water Study, was mailed to each of you.

My credentials are as follows:

1.1960-62,Chairman,Nuclear and Radiological Defense Committee,US Army Chemical Corp School.

2.1962,Dept. of Defense Radiological Safety Officer,Nevada Test Site

3. 1964,Retirement from US Army as Instructor, Nuclear Weapons Instructor, MOS 8 7330.

4. 1966-68, Pinellas County Health Dept, evaluated radiation from watch repair facilities,color televisions,microwave ovens,and dental facilities(cited by Harvard University).

5 1968-9,Consultant, US Bureau of Radiological Health.

6 1970,BS degree in Engineering,Energy Conversion.

7. 1971-2,Supervisor, Licensing and Regulatory Affairs,Florida Power Corp.,during planning,licensing,and construction of a nuclear power reactor.

8.1990, Nuclear Effects Advisor to the movie,"Blue Sky".

Only current radiological sampling of the CAP water and the Avra Valley-CAP blend can negate the conclusions contained in the above cited report sent to you. In view of the sixty Tucson Water Dept.monitoring violations cited by USEPA and previously mentioned in a 5 July,2008, communication to you, reliability of results can best be assured by an independant sampling and evaluation labratory for water and sediments in water.

Respectfully. Clyde H. Stagner, a Tucson citizen

5

EPA Home   Envirofacts   SDWIS

SDWIS Violation Report

TUCSON WATER-CATALINA

TUCSON, AZ 85726-7210

520-791-5256

Primary Water Source Type	Population Served
Groundwater	1200

This report was created on MAY-25-2008
Results are based on data extracted on APR-15-2008

NOTICE: EPA is aware of inaccuracies and underreporting of some data in the Safe Drinking Water Information System. We are working with the states to improve the quality of the data.

The tables below list all violations that the state reported to EPA for this water system. Health-based violations are listed first, followed by monitoring, reporting, and other violations.

Health Based Violations: amount of contaminant exceeded safety standard (MCL) or water was not treated properly.
No health-based violations found. EPA has no record of any health-based violations reported by the state for this water system (Violations within last 10 years are included in this report).

Monitoring and Reporting and Other Violations: system failed to complete all samples or sample in a timely manner, or had another non-health-based violation. A significant monitoring violation means the system failed to take a large percentage of the required samples. Non-significant monitoring violations indicate that the water system failed to take some of the required samples, but did do some of the required sampling.

Type of Violation	Sampling Period: Begin Date	Sampling Period End Date	Contaminant	Violation ID
Follow-up and Routine Tap Sampling	OCT-01-2006	DEC-31-2025	Lead & Copper Rule	1725

No follow-up action has been reported to EPA for this violation. Please contact the state drinking water program for more information.

Type of Violation	Sampling Period: Begin Date	Sampling Period End Date	Contaminant	Violation ID
Monitoring, Routine Minor (TCR)	FEB-01-2006	FEB-28-2006	Coliform (TCR)	1706

From:	"cstampingr@dakotacom.net" <cstamping@dakotacom.net>
To:	<Owens.Stephen@azdeq.gov>
Sent:	Friday, April 18, 2008 2:33 PM
Subject:	Tucson water system violations

Dear Mr. Owrens:

The EPA lists 32 violations ,among EPA Violation #`s 205478 and 205451, in 2007 by the Tucson Water System wiyhout resolution.The EPA advises contacting the State Drinking Water Program to determine resolution of these violations.

Accordingly,I requested the resolutions from Ms.Joan Card on 16 Apr 08. A response has not been received. Accordingly, I am requesting the resolution details of these violations from you.

Respectfully,
Clyde H Stagner
8565 Pembrook Drive
Tucson Az 85715

From:	"cstampingr@dakotacom.net" <cstamping@dakotacom.net>
To:	<mcweb@tucsonaz.gov>
Sent:	Thursday, April 24, 2008 3:43 PM
Subject:	Tucson Water System Violations

Dear Honorable Council Persons,

A very recent perusal of EPA`s list of violations revealed 32 monitoring violations in 2007 by Tucson Water System.These violations are among those listed from Violation #205478 to Violation #205451,inclusively. For resolution of these nonresolvsed violations,the EPA refers to the Azdeq.gov.

Emails, seeking resolution(fines,et al) of these Violations,were sent to Joan Card and Stephen Owens at Azdeq.gov, and to the Tucson Water System at   . To date no response has been received.

This citizen of Tucson requests that you obtain the Resolutions to these Monitoring Violations and advise the undersigned of penalties imposed on the Tucson Water System to include the name(s) of individuals responsible and/ or accountable. Also please cite the actions taken by Tucson Water System to preclude future recurrences.

Clyde H. Stagner: 8565 Pembrook Drive
Tucson, Az 85715

From:	"cstampingr@dakotacom.net" <cstamping@dakotacom.net>
To:	<dbradley@azleg.gov>
Sent:	Sunday, May 11, 2008 9:17 AM
Subject:	Tucson Drinking Water

Dear Honorable Representative David Bradley,

On 5 May 2008,the USEPA listed 63 drinking water monitoring violations in its Safe Drinking Water Information System(SDWIS). The information for listing these drinking water monitoring violations was submitted to USEPA by thr Arizona Department of Environmental Quality. Sir efforts to view these violations and the administrative protocol there for ,on the ADEQ website , have met with ADEQ control of information not to be released to other parties in contradistinction to the Arizona open government protocol.

The statement that EPA makes concerning no drinking water standards violations by Tucson Water System is misleading. The drinking water monitoring violations cited above for which samples were not taken,or were lost, could have contaminant levels from zero to levels greater than the Maximum Contaminant Levels(MCL) established by USEPA. What is in the water the citizens and children of Tucson are drinking? Request your effort to open this USEPA<ADEQ<Tucson Water System protocol and results therefrom to the citizens of Tucson in accordance with the Arizona open government law contained in the Arizona Revised Statutes.

Respectfully, clyde h stagner,a citizen of Tucson

From: "cstampingr@dakotacom.net" <cstamping@dakotacom.net>
To: "Remy Sawyer" <Remy.Sawyer@tucsonaz.gov>
Sent: Monday, April 28, 2008 2:44 PM
Subject: Re: Tucson Water's Response to 2007 EPA List of Issues

Dear Remy Sawyer,
  Thank you for response. If the violations first reported to AZDEQ and EPA
were not violations,why were they reported as violations in the first place?
A violation is a violation or a false report of a violation. In any
event,someone is resposible and accountable but apparently isn`t being held
accountable or resposibility. The correction of Violation #205451 is
understood as you ezplained. However.an entry of "corrected" in the
EPA(instead of deleted) Violation List would be a more accurate
representation of fact .
  Why were each of the other cited violations of 2007 cleared by ADEQ?
  Again,thank you for your respose-Sincerely,Clyde H. Stagner----- Original
Message -----
From: "Remy Sawyer" <Remy. Sawyer a tucsonaz.gov >
To: <cstamping a dakotacom.net>
Sent: Monday, April 28, 2008 1:19 PM
Subject: Tucson Water's Response to 2007 EPA List of Issues

Hello Mr. Stagner,
Thank you for your recent inquiry regarding EPA's list of monitoring
violations that occurred in 2007, specifically Violation ID 205451 through
205478. Referencing EPA's Safe Drinking Water Information System (SDWIS)
Violation Report and touching base with the Arizona Department of
Environmental Quality (ADEQ)for their input regarding this Report, the
current status of these violations is as follows. But first, I thought it
may be beneficial to provide some background information.

Background
Tucson Water reports compliance data to ADEQ (our regulator for the state of
Arizona)to ensure compliance with the regulatory drinking water
requirements. ADEQ uploads our compliance data, as well as compliance
status information, to EPA's SDWIS database, where the public can view the
information.

The majority of the entries in SDWIS do not accurately reflect the
compliance status for Tucson Water and we, as well as other systems
regulated by ADEQ, have been working with ADEQ to address the issue of
mistaken violations in the uploaded data. With the help of ADEQ, nearly all
of the Tucson Water non-compliance issues in SDWIS have been correctly
changed back to compliance. Although the violations are cleared by ADEQ,
unfortunately the SDWIS database is updated only a few times per year and so
what is posted on SDWIS is not current or does not accurately reflect the
situation.

From: "cstampingr@dakotacom.net" <cstamping@dakotacom.net>
To: <mcweb@tucsonaz.gov>
Sent: Tuesday, May 06, 2008 4:03 PM
Subject: Tucson Water System Monitoring Violations

Honorable Mayor an Councilpersons:

The USEPA cites the following Tucson Water System sources:Catalina(1200 people served),Corona (6000),Diamond Bell(723),Rancho Del Sol Lindo(3102),Sunset Ranch(45),Thunderhead Ranch(171),Valley View (474),Sierrita Foothills(87),and Tucson Water System(675,000). USEPA cites 520 791-5256 as the telephone reference no. for these nine water sources which are included within their Safe Drinking Water Information System(SDWIS).

USEPA established Maximum Contaminant Levels(MCL) for contaminants,usually in parts per billion. A groundwater source violation for which required sampling was not done,or the loss of samples taken therefrom,is misleading because the contaminant could have been any measured amount from zero to a level in excess of the MCL-which would be a health- based violation. USEPA has no record of any health-based violations reported by the State of Az(AZDEQ) within the last ten years.

Cause for concern for failure to monitor drinking water as specified by USEPA arises from my wife`s medical condition.In 1992,her cancerous left kidney was completely removed(in Tucson). In 2002,radical colon cancer removal resulted in a colestemy;a stent from the bottom of her remaining kidney to the top of her bladder which is surgically removed and replaced every nine months;a remaining right kidney functioning at 18%,or less; an AV fistula on her right arm in preparation for dialysis; a dissecting, descending aneruysm from the top of the aorta to kidney level;pleurisy;depression;arthritis;three hour nap daily;and 8-12 hours of 2-liter oxygen overnight.

SDWISreports groundwater violation reports to include thebnine Tucso Water sources listed previously. The May-04-2008 listed violations were based on data extracted on Apr-15-2008. Their violations table lists all violations that the state(AZDEQ) reported to the EPA for the Tucson Water System:Catalina(3):Corona (5);Diamond Bell(3);Rancho Del Sol Lindo(1);Sierrita Foothills(1);Sunset Ranch(0); Thunderhead Ranch(0);Valley View(4): Tucson Water System(63).

The USEPA SDWIS Violation Report for Tucson Water-Thunderhead Ranch is of interest.
Seventy One Follow-up Actions were done by the Tucson Water System to accomplish"St Compliance Achieved" with zero violations. Monitoring tests were done for 25 contaminants of the water source servicing 171 persons. Many of these same contaminants are still listed as violations in the Tucson Water System servicing 675,000 persons.

In fiscal year 2005,based on information reported to the USEPA by the states, 98.5% of all systems reported no treatment technique violations, 93.9% of all systems reported no MCL violations,and 76 % of all systems reported no reporting/monitoring violations. Attempts were made,without success, to ascertain person(s) or governmental entities responsible and accountable for the Tucson Water System monitoring violations-necessary designations to elicit corrective action.

Consequently,you, the elected leaders of Tucson, are requested to take the necessary action to cause the Tucson Water System to expeditiously accomplish the Follow-uo Action of drinking water monitoring and future inclusion of the Tucson Water System in the per cent of all systems reporting no reporting/monitoring violations. This action is requested to possibly benefit the health my wife,and for the benefit of the citizens of Tucson,especially the young and elderly.

Respectfully,Clyde H Stagner, a citizen of Tucson

From:	"cstampingr@dakotacom.net" <cstamping@dakotacom.net>
To:	<mcweb@tucsonaz.gov>
Sent:	Friday, April 25, 2008 9:26 AM
Subject:	Priveleged Group within Society

Dear Honorable Tucson Council Members,

On April 24,2008,an email from Mr. John Calkins,Manager,Drinking Water Section, ADEQ,was appreciatively received. The email contained information concerning Tucson Water System monitoring violations.

The bottom of the email contained the following " Notice:This e-mail(and any attachments)may contain PRIVILEGED OR CONFIDENTIAL information and is intended only for the use of the specific individual(s) to whom it is addressed.It may contain information that is priveleged and confidential under state and federal law. This information may be used or disclosed only in accordance with law, and you may be subject to penalties under law for improper use or further disclosure of the information in this email and its attachments. If you have received this email in error,please immediately notify the person named above by reply e-mail, and the delete the original e-mail. Thank you."

Honorable Council Members,what is so secrative about Tucson Water Systems monitoring violations. Who suffers if these water monitoring violations are released to the public- the citizens of Tucson or the Tucson Water System? The Notice cited above is tangled with a multiplicity of censorship controls-to whom does the recipient apply to obtain permission to disclose or seek removal of this censorship secrecy shroud? State and federal law requiring sequesturing of information must,and should be,adhered to-why are not these laws specifically cited for the email received? The US Government,by law, must submit unclassified information to a requestor under the "FREEDOM OF INFORMATION ACT". The EPA has no restrictions on their citation of the Tucson Water Systems monitoring violations.

This Letter of Citizen Concern finds no wrong,or fault, with Mr. John Calkins,Manager,Drinking Water Section,ADEQ, who is accomplishing his responsibilities according to protocol.

Clyde H Stagner,
8565 Pembrook Drive
Tucsom,Az   85715

From:	"cstampingr@dakotacom.net" <cstamping@dakotacom.net>
To:	<TW_Web1@tucsonaz.gov>
Cc:	<TW_Web6@tucsonaz.gov>
Sent:	Friday, May 30, 2008 8:22 AM
Subject:	TW Webmail

Dear Tucson Water Dept.,

On Page 8,2007,your Annual Water Quality Report under,"Whom do I contact for more information?" reads:
"In 2007, Tucson Water also collected a large amount of additional monthly water quality data.. The results of this additional monitoring are available on the Tucson Water web site,www.tucson.gov/water/."

On this date,30 May 2008, the additional water monitoring data cited by Tucson Water,supra, was nonexistant, unavailable, or unaccessable on the internet.

Please advise of specific internet address(es) where Tucson Water additional monthly water quality data,cited supra, can be accessed.

Sincerely,clyde h stagner,resident and taxpayer in Tucson

From:	<info@tucsonpimawaterstudy.com>
To:	<cstamping@dakotacom.net>
Sent:	Wednesday, May 21, 2008 12:48 PM
Subject:	Re: email

Dear Mr. Stagner:

Thank you for your comments and interest in the joint City/Tucson Water Study. This email is being forwarded to Oversight Committee members and staff at Tucson Water and Pima County Regional Wastewater Reclamation Departments for response.

Thank you.

Comments/Questions: Dear Oversight Committee Members,   21 May,2008

Joint Tucson/Pima water planning can be beneficial to residents of both populations.
Before unveiling a crystal ball for the future, however, please ascertain the present operational health of the Tucson Water System, the Pima County Wastewater Management, and the Solid Waste Management Department. Most assuredly, Committee Members, the future water fix is based on the present water fix. As population pours into the Tucson funnel, the funnel exit must accomodate human effluent and solid waste to avoid catastrophic impacts on the population. Accordingly,disaster plans, in the future, develop from the disaster plans,natural and human, in existance today. Committee Members,before embarking on this daunting task, can you attest to the present adequacy and proficiency of the Tucson/Pima governmental entities?
>   Why, on 5 May, 2008,were there 63 drinking water monitoring violations and 2 CCR violations cited by the USEPA ENVIROFACTS whereas 76 % of the drinking water systems in the US have no drinking water monitoring violations. What enforcement action,to eliminate violations,has Arizona Department of Environmental Quality implemented?
>   Why does USEPA-ECHO show Pima County Wastewater Management Ina Road,AZ 0020001, with six(6) quarters in nocompliance with seven(7) inspections-other Pima County Wastewater Management Programs are listed.
>   Committee Members, does the Tucson Water System have a viable man-made disaster response and recovery plan in print,included in a master Response Plan, and operationally acceptable to the Emergency Operations Accountable and Responsiblity personnel of Tucson/Pima (and who are these individuals by name?
>   Sincerely,clyde h stagner,a citizen of Tucson and Pima Co.

11

From: "cstampingr@dakotacom.net" <cstamping@dakotacom.net>
To: "Mohsen Belyani" <Mohsen.Belyani@tucsonaz.gov>
Sent: Sunday, June 08, 2008 6:49 PM
Subject: Fw: Sustainable Water Quality

Info-clyde stagner
----- Original Message -----
From: cstampingr@dakotacom.net
To: mcweb@tucsonaz.gov
Sent: Sunday, June 08, 2008 4:48 PM
Subject: Sustainable Water Quality

Dear Honorable Council Members,
Water testing by Tucson Water Dept in 2000 resulted in:

Water System	Radon:pCi/L	2- 1/2 lives later
Coronado de Tucson	1604	401
Diamond Bell	864	216
Rancho De Sol Lindo	1033	258
Thunderhead	356	89
Valley View	789	197
Tucson	1420	355

The levels cited above were maximum levels measured-remaining wells measured equal,or less ,per liter. The recommended standard for drinking water,by the American Academy of Science and USEPA is 300 pCi/l. The half life of radon is 3.825 days. Two half lives, or 7.65 days, results in the pCi/l shown in column three,above. Transit time from wellhead to user would consume more time and urther lessen the levels cited in column three above.

For new developments(homeowners will protect their children) require venting underground potable water storage tanks capable of storing I15 GPD X 7days= 805 gallons for a Tucson Water Dept.`s previously measured 1600 pCi/L and adjustments made to lesser tank volumes for lesser measured radon levels. An alternative would be a larger tank,installed by the developer,for the entire development.

Tucson Water Dept can further the effort,over time, by increasing the time for water flow with venting enroute to user

This methodology would also make available local emergency water supplies in case of natural or manmade disasters.Its applicability for fire fighting is at the discretion of the given fire department.

That USEPA does not have a standard for radon in drinking water does not relieve elected leaders from their responsibility to protect their citizens from a recognized hazard to their health

Respectfully.Clyde H Stagner, a Tucson citizen

From:	"cstampingr@dakotacom.net" <cstamping@dakotacom.net>
To:	<mcweb@tucsonaz.gov>
Sent:	Saturday, July 05, 2008 11:17 AM
Subject:	Tucson Water Monitoring Violations

Honerable Mayor and Council Members,

The USEPA Safe Drinking Water Infomation System(SDWIS) lists the following ID drinking water monitoring violations by Tucson Water:

205451	36204
204452	36304
205479-205489,inclusive	36404
205455	36504
205457-205463,inclusive	36604
205466	36704
205467	36804
205469-205478,inclusive	36904
205539-205541,inclusive	35004
205468	35104
205538-205532,inclusive	35204
35304	302
35404	
35504	
35604	
35704	
35804	
35904	
36004	
36104	

In addition,two CCR Violation ID`s are204806 and 204706.This USEPA Report was created on July 4, 2008 based on data extracted on 4 April, 2008.

In the United States,76% of the potable water systems do not have any violations.Monitoring for contaminants assures(hopefully) delivery of healthy potable water. Failure to monitor is the antithesis.

As our elected leaders,please exercise your authority to correct these monitoring violations for the health and welfare of my family and the families of Tucson.

Respectfully,Clyde H Stagner,a Tucson citizen

Dear Honorable Tucson Pima Water Study Members,   17 Sept 08

Both Julia Fonseca and Rob Marshall, ~~our~~ the presenters today, have

years of scientific experience. Their ecological and aquifer

monitoring requirements are essential elements to the

scientific predictability process. For example, the scientific

monitoring and repeat monitoring of Hurricane Ike resulted in the

predictability of landfall, wind speeds, rainfall, tornados, water

surge, and other parameters- all necessary for survivability of

human life, an organism of the environment. Survivability is a

prerequisite of sustainability. Our presenters today need

environmental monitoring data to predict the actions necessary for

the survivability and sustainability of the flora and fauna in the

natural environmental areas of Tucson, Pima County and

associated areas. There are no maximum concentration limits

(MCL) in their horizon-only survivability and sustainability over

the short term and long term. They are caregivers for our natural

14

areas.

The people of Tucson are environmental organisms. Tertiary treated Las Vegas wastewater contains perchlorates , pharmaceuticals, radioactive materials, sediments, and several other pollutants, all of which concerned the Governor` s Clean Colorado River Alliance who recommend follow up action. The citizens of Tucson are drinking diluted pollutant contaminated Las Vegas wastewater in the CAP bled distributed by the Tucson Water Department. Monitoring is a necessary and essential precursor for the determination of mandatory abatement or avoidance levels of contaminants. There is no higher authority limiting monitoring by the Tucson Water Department.

Can the poverty people of Tucson afford bottled water?

Is your child drinking bottled water?

Are you drinking bottled water?

Who are the caregivers for the citizens of Tucson?

Respectfully,Clyde H Stagner,a citizen of Tucson and Pima Co.

From: cstampingr@dakotacom.net
To: Ursula Kramer
Sent: Sat May 03 11:37:58 2008
Subject: Fw: Water Monitoring Violations

Dear Ursula Kramer,
   The Tucson Water System Has 32 monitoring violations, for 2007, listed by EPA. resolution of accountability and responsibility has yet to be ascertained. A first effort to do so followed EPA instructions by contacting ADEQ . ADEQ`s response is ,incontradistinction to your openness, sequestured with censorship,privelegedness,and violation of restrictive guards if the contents of the email to me were opened to another.
   Apparently. the administrative,and chain of order,protocol is detrimental to the Tucson Water System according to Remy Sawyer. Several Tucson Water System water monitoring Violations,ID# 3547,and from 205451 <mailto:from 205451> through 205467, noninclusively, have been deleted by print in an additional format column behind the Violation columns which remain in print.
   Either the Violations are correctly listed by EPA and/or erroneously submitted to EPA by ADEQ. Who is responsible and accountable?
   Your acumen is solicited for resolution of this paradox.
        Sincerely,
        Clyde H Stagner,a citizen of Tucson
From: cstampingr@dakotacom.net
To: Remy Sawyer <mailto:Remy Sawyer@tucsonaz.gov>
Cc: Ward2 Ward2 <mailto:Ward2@tucsonaz.gov>
Sent: Tuesday, April 29, 2008 11:24 AM
Subject: Water Monitoring Violations

Dear Mr. Sawyer,
  Thank you for the Tucson Water Monitoring Violations explanation from the Tucson Water Systems involvement.
  EPA`s SDWIS cites three(3) Violation Status Actions:
            Cancelled-action not performed.
            Complete-the action was performed.
            Reported-action was reported to EPA.

  Reconciliation of the Tucson Water Violations with these Violation Status Actions is difficult,if not impossible,even with your extensive explanation and elaboration which was helpful.
  Since there is a governmental chain of order(TWS>ADEQ>EPA)acknowledgement and verification of itemized irresponsibility by ADEQ is a necessary substantiation of your explanation.
  The comments rendered herein are by no means to be construed as degrading to Mr. Sawyers comments or performance of duties.
   Thanks again-clyde h stagner-a Tucson citizen

cstampingr@dakotacom.net

From: "cstampingr@dakotacom.net" <cstamping@dakotacom.net>
To: <ombuds@azoca.gov>
Sent: Tuesday, May 06, 2008 10:48 AM
Subject: Fw: Water Monitoring Violations

Dear Sir,
  Please advise ADEQ to remove the unreferenced Priveleged and confidential threat with censor ship inuendo contained in the notice at the end of the included email from ADEQ.
  Sincerely,Clyde H Stagner,a citizen of Tucson
----- Original Message -----
From: John A. Calkins
To: cstampingr@dakotacom.net
Sent: Monday, May 05, 2008 7:58 AM
Subject: RE: Water Monitoring Violations

Mr. Stager:

As outlined in my 04/24/2008 email correspondence to you, state updates and/or modifications to the 2007 violations will likely take six or more months to be reflected in EPA's Envirofacts. Our next upload will occur no later than March 15, 2008

Sincerely,

John Calkins, Manager
Drinking Water Section
Arizona Department of Environmental Quality
p: (602) 771-4617
f: (602) 771-4634
calkins.john@azdeq.gov

From: cstampingr@dakotacom.net [mailto:cstamping@dakotacom.net]
Sent: Sunday, May 04, 2008 8:26 AM
To: John A. Calkins
Subject: Fw: Water Monitoring Violations

Dear Mr. Calkins,
  Explanations of the Tucson Water System 2007 water monitoring violations listed by EPA have failed
to designate the resposibile and accountable government entity and individual(s) with indications ADEQ may be responsible.
  Enclosed are applicable references.
  Request an open dialogue response from a tax supported Arizona government agency,ADEQ, to
      Clyde H Stagner,a tax paying Tucson citizen.
----- Original Message -----
From: Ursula Kramer
To: cstamping@dakotacom.net
Sent: Sunday, May 04, 2008 7:07 AM
Subject: Re: Water Monitoring Violations

Pima County does not regulate Tucson Water. That authority rests with the State ADEQ. I would recommend you contact the state water program for further information.

CHAPTER 3

CENTRAL ARIZONA PROJECT (CAP)

Over the years, the Tucson aquifer level dropped in one area by 200 feet due to removal of water annually in excess of the annual natural groundwater replenishment of approximately 60,000 acre-ft. The Water Conservation Division Groundwater Management Act of 1980 specifies achieving zero overdraft by 2025. To recharge the aquifer and to balance the aquifer annual drawdown, additional sources of water were needed. In the 1970s Tucson purchased farmlands in Avra Valley which provide approximately 17,500 acre-ft of natural recharge annually. In addition, Tucson received a CAP allocation which ultimately reached 144,000 acre-ft annually. In 2025, Tucson`s annual available water inventory shall be the sum of these sources equal to 211,500 acre-ft-unless additional sources are obtained.

The CAP surface water begins in the upper Colorado River Basin from whence it flows through Utah and its adjacent uranium mining operations. After flowing across northern Arizona, the Colorado River enters Lake Mead behind Hoover Dam. Las Vegas and Henderson, Nev., withdraw water from Lake Mead, treat it, distribute potable water, collect and treat the wastewater before discharging the wastewater, via the Las Vegas Wash, into Lake Mead-their wastewater treatment plants cannot completely remove all contaminants. In production facilities along the Las Vegas Wash several decades ago, rocket propellant, involving perchlorate, was produced. The facilities ceased operation before a disastrous fire spread the per chlorate residue with subsequent increases in per chlorate contamination in the Las Vegas Wash, Lake Mead, and all points in the Lower Colorado River and its distribution systems south of Hoover Dam.

At Topock, between Hoover Dam and the Colorado River Cap Havisu intake, the USGS measured radioactive contamination in 1981 and 1986. The CAP delivery system, for Colorado River surface water, is a 336 mile canal from the Havisu Intake , through central Arizona to Phoenix, and thence to an end terminal 14 miles southwest of Tucson. In 1992, the Tucson Water Department began piping CAP water directly to 84,000 homes with disastrous results. The Total Dissolved Solids (TDS) in CAP water were double that of the groundwater in the Tucson area. By 1994, the CAP water effectively scoured older pipes and damaged home appliances resulting in approximately 5,000 damage claims against the City of Tucson The citizens of Tucson passed Proposition 200, the Water Consumer Protection Act of 1995. This Act required recharge to the aquifer with water quality stipulations.

The Avra Valley Project for recharge of CAP surface water was permitted, with quality and quantity specifications, to CAWAD by the Arizona Department of Water Resources (ADWR). Delivery of Clearwater blend water to Tucson began in 2001. The untreated Cap water at the Clearwater site (Avra Valley) had a maximum of 0.064 mg/L of lead whereas the USEPA MCL is 0.015 mg/L-for fourteen samples the Mean of 0.051 + the Standard Deviation equaled 0.0221 mg/L. In May ,2006, the Central Arizona Project CAP Canal Water Quality report cited 2.3 ug/L of per chlorates in CAP water at the San Xavier Pumping Plant. The Tucson Water Dept.

,in its 2007 Annual Water Quality Report, cites a 55% blend of native groundwater and 45% recharged CAP water which, over time, will contain an increasing percentage of recharged CAP water. The TDS in the blend also increases as the CAP percentage increases. The Tucson Water Dept. is not responsible for the concentration of TDS in Tucson` s drinking water - the Tucson elected city council is responsible and without a limit on the TDS per liter, the City of Tucson can expect future claims for degradation of water pipe and home appliances.

In 2005, the Governor of Arizona appointed noted experts to the Clean Colorado River Alliance which submitted recommendations for action by the Governor and other leaders for improvement of water quality in the Colorado River. Their pollutant concerns consisted of:

 1. Nutrients(nitrogen, nitrates, ammonia, phosphorus)
 2. Metals (Cr, Ur, Se,)
 3. Endocrine disrupting compounds
 4. Perchlorate
 5. Bacteria/pathogens
 6. Salinity/ total dissolved solids
 7. Sediment/turbidity

Research resulted in a conclusion of no action taken by state, county, or municipal governments concerning the pollutants listed above.

A USGS study of selected fish in Lake Mead found sexual changes in male fish die to contaminants, individual or synergistically.

8565 Pembrook Drive
Tucson, AZ 85715

18 June 2008

Subject: Tucson and CAP

Dear Honorable Tucson Council Members,
 Mayor Bob Walkup
 Ward One Regina Romero
 Ward Two Rodney Glassman
 Ward Three Karen Uhlich
 Ward Four Shirley Scott
 Ward Five Steve Leal
 Vice Mayor, Ward Six Nina J. Trasoff

   Population growth along the lower Colorado River Basin has been explosive with the Colorado River watershed built on septic tanks with nitrates seeping into a watershed that threatens not only residents, but also the drinking water supply of all of Arizona and California (Ref: Statement of Terrence L. Bracy to Ms. Card and members of the Clean Colorado River Alliance, "On Federal Role in Protecting Water Quality: a National Perspective", June 17, 2005). There is also the issue of the poisonous residue of the rocket fuel ingredient perchlorate (can interfere with thyroid function) seeping at a rate of 400 pounds a day from a former government facility in Henderson, Nevada. Near Moab, Utah, a now closed uranium mine left behind a pile of radioactive waste that covers 130 acres, is 94 feet tall, and sits 750 feet from the Colorado River in a flood plain and is responsible for an estimated 110,000 gallons of radioactive groundwater seeping into the Colorado River each day (Ref: supra).
   A short article from the Salt Lake Tribune regarding the U.S. Department of Energy`s recent release of a request for proposals for the cleanup of the Moab uranium mill tailings site which included the removal of nearly 12 million tons of radioactive tailings and moving them approximately thirty miles north to a repository near Crescent, Utah (Ref: Executive Director`s Monthly Report to the Colorado River Board of California, Nov. 14,2006 and signed by Gerald B. Zimmerman, Executive Director).On July 17,2005, it was disclosed that DOE`s funding cycle for the next five years was insufficient to move the pile (Ref: LR Press Release, Sept 1, 2006, Scientists reveal a higher discharge and frequency of extreme floods along the Colorado River).
   The amount of money being spent to close dangerous mines is miniscule compared to that being spent by Congress to clean up defunct uranium mills. The most costly of the cleanups could be the Atlas site where 10,000 tons of contaminated soils are currently leaking into the Colorado River. DOE has already funded cleanup of four uranium mills in Utah and 20 other mills around the West. Scores of smaller, privately owned mills remain lost and forgotten in the canyons of southern Utah where each rainfall carries the

radioactive sediments into the local streams, and ultimately, into the Colorado River (Ref: Uranium mining left a legacy of death, Desert news.com, by Jerry D. Spangler and Donna Kemp Spangler, Feb. 13, 2001).

In an effort to better understand the impact from extreme floods on the infrastructure and water resources of the Colorado River corridor, Living Rivers, supported by a grant from the Citizen` s Monitoring and Technical Assessment Fund, commissioned two flood studies in Utah near the town of Moab. Two critical issues were examined:

1. River mitigation adjacent to the second largest uranium waste pile in the United States.

2. The magnitude and frequency of large floods along the Colorado River.

The mitigation was performed by two professors of geology from the University of Arizona: John C. Dohrnwend and Noam Greenbaum. A conclusion was that previous investigation by the Department of Energy (DOE) failed to provide reasonable assurances that the radioactive waste pile in Utah was safe from probable maximum floods within the next 1,000 years, a reclamation standard DOE is required to fulfill under USEPA regulations. The result of a pale flood study completed in June, 2006, by Greenbaum, provided evidence to support a conclusion that floods occurring at 100, and 500, year intervals in the Colorado River Basin are not properly understood and shows that catastrophic floods can occur with much greater frequency than originally speculated and that such floods could happen"sooner as opposed to later".

The Las Vegas Wash is an excavated waterway channel which drains all surface water and effluent discharge from sewage treatment facilities from the greater Las Vegas Metropolitan Area to Lake Mead. Fine and course sediment samples were collected at 100 meter intervals and analyzed to determine the distribution of gamma-emitting radionuclides in the lower 5,500 meters of the Las Vegas Wash. Results indicated long-lived fission products in up stream Wash sediments. However, trace levels of CS-137 measured in downstream sediment suggested the suspension and transport of radioactive fallout within the Wash. Levels of K-40, Th-232, U-235, U-238 found in the Wash sediment were consistent with levels typically found in southeast Nevada soils (Ref: Radionuclide content of Las Vegas Wash sediments, by M.J.Rudin, W.H.Johnson, and A.M.Meyers ,Chemosphere, Volume 35, Issue 12 , Dec. 1997,pages 3039-3046).

Since the start of a persistent drought around the year 2000, inflows to Lake Powell on the Colorado River have been below average, leading to drawdown of Lake Mead and Lake Powell, the primary means of storage on the river. Drought has a multiyear character and may persist for several decades-four droughts have occurred lasting more than twenty years (Ref: USGS Climate Flutcuations, Drought and Flow of the Colorado River).The drought conditions in Arizona over the last several years has depleted water available for surface water as well as groundwater recharge (Ref: US Geological Survey Fact Sheet 2005-3081).

Data on the radium content of bottom sediment material collected in 1960 and 1961 throughout the Colorado River Basin is provided in" Colorado River Basin Radioactive

Materials, OSTI ID-7215422". Radon derived from the diffusion of bottom sediments is an important component of the radon budget in the surface water at Honan South located in Southern Australia, but does not account for all the radon (Ref: Internet: iah.org,au.pdfs/white).

There are two sites on the Colorado River that are near, or upstream, from the entry point to the Central Arizona Project (CAP) canal that have radionuclide data (Ref: email from Cheryl Partin, Az QW Data Administrator-email attached). The two sites of 1981 ,and 1986, data are:

USGS 09424000   Colorado River near Toprock, AZ
USGS 09423000   Colorado River below Davis Dam, AZ-NV

With monitoring results:

Sample ID	Description	Maximum Measured
P09510	Alpha-emitting isotope of radium	0.2 pCi/L
P80030	Gross alpha radioactivity,uranium	<3.5 µg/L
P03515	Gross beta radioactivity,Cs-137 curve	4.6 pCi/L
P80050	Gross beta activity	3.5 pCi/L
P82068	Potassium-40, average	3.5 pCi/L
P22703	Uranium,natural	4.3 µg/L
P80040	Gross alpha,suspended sediment,U curve	<0.7 µg/L
P03516	Gross beta,suspended sediment, Cs curve	2.0 pCi/L
P80060	Gross beta,suspended sediment,Sr/Y curve	2.1 pCi/L

The sample results shown are subject to the considerations contained in " National Water Quality Laboratory Technical Memorandum 96-11",dated June 6,1996 which eliminated citing a curve in the results shown and stipulates the the curve citation does not necessarily indicate the presence of that element(s) in the measured results.

USEPA states in its guidance (Ref: Federal Register, October 23, 2003, Volume 68, Number 205) that "watershed-based plans should address not only the sources of water quality impairment, but also any pollutants and souces of pollutants that need to be addressed to assure the long-term health of the watershed, including both surface and groundwater that serve as sources of drinking water". The Pima Association of Governments (PAG) cites the above in the endorsements and involvements by the Arizona Department of Environmental Quality (Ref: Watershed Approach to Water Quality Management Planning,pagnet.org/document/water/PC208/ch8_Apr06).*This paragraph requires watershed pollutants to be monitored in absence of a USEPA established MCL standard.*

The CAP Water Quality program consists of scheduled grab samples at various designated locations along the canal system from Lake Havasu to San Xavier pumping station. The permitting process and regulatory compliance for the Avra Valley Recharge Project,Lower Santa Cruz Recharge Project and the Pima Mine Road Recharge Project requires quarterly monitoring with the data results compiled into an annual report and made a matter of public record. The 2007 CAP water quality monitoring data results do not include any pollutants containing radioactivity which are needed to address the long-term watershed health advocated by AZDEQ and required by USEPA.

Tucson has rights to 144,000 acre-feet of Cap water annually.CAP water contains significant quantities of dissolved solids(TDS), which in large concentrations can affect the taste of drinking water and adversely affect plumbing. Water with TDS concentrations of less than 500 mg/L-about a quarter of a teaspoon of salts per gallon of water-generally is suited for most uses(Ref: USGS, Arizona, FS 170-98). USEPA has established 500 mg/L as the MCLG for TDS as the most acceptable aesthetic concentration. Tucson Water Department is committed to 450 mg/L for the foreseeable future (Ref: Tucson Water,Total Dissolved Solids). The TDS effects on water taste, on plumbing, and on build up of terrestrial salts on home lots(gray water) and effluent deposition areas is cause for a Tucson City Code specification for allowable, enforceable, and acceptable TDS in potable drinking water and a Pima County specification for waste water effluent .

At the end of 2007, Tucson water was using approximately 62% of its available allocation of CAP water(Ref: Tucson Water 2007 Annual Water Quality Report) in a blend of drinking water which contained about 55% native groundwater and 45% recharged Colorado River water from Avra Valley. In 2006,average of Cap TDS grab sample concentration was 663 mg/L and the average monthly TDS concentration at the San Xavier Pumping Station was 663 mg/L.

In 1994, existing Tucson Water Avra Valley supply wells had a TDS of 210 mg/L(Ref: Appendix B,Tucson Water,Water Quality Data,Malcolm Pirnie, August,1944).

CAVSARP blend recovery is ramping up to 70,000 acre-feet a year(Ref: Tucson Water, CAVSARP facilities). Of the 70,000 acre-feet, 45% is CAP equaling 31,500 acre-feet annually with the remaining 55%, 38,500 acre-feet, being ground water.

For 100 liters of blended water:

$$45L \times 663mg/L + 55L \times 210\ mg/L = 41385\ mg/100L = 413.85\ mg/L$$

Which differs from the Tucson Water June 8, 2008, Clearwater Quality Report of 372.5 mg/L.

Avra Valley net aquifer storage fom spring 2002 to spring 2004 was 70,000 acre-feet net storage increase (some may be due to nearby recharge)(Ref: Groundwater Users Advisory Council Minutes,Azwater.gov)..This natural recharge of 35,000 acre feet exceeds the 38,500 acre-feet required for the 55% groundwater contribution.

A water blend 64% CAP and 36 % Avra Valley groundwater fot the daily 70,000 acre-feet drinking water blend gives a TDS of:

$$64L \times 663\ mg/L + 36L \times 210\ mg/L = 49992\ mg/100L = 499.92 \sim 500\ mg/L$$

Which is the USEPA aesthetic standard for TDS. This mix results annually in:

0.64 x 70000 Total acre-feet = 44,800 Cap acre-feet ,and
0.36 x 70,000 Total acre-feet = 25,200 acre-feet Avra Valley Groundwater

The 25,200acre-feet of Avra Valley groundwater for blend is less than the 35,000 acre-feet of natural recharge. Additional blend from Avra Valley may be wanted in the year 2025.

A contaminat in the Avra Valley ground water, which is not present in the CAP water, is reduced by a factor of 0.36 in the blend:

Wellhead	1999,Radon,pCi/L	Blend,pCi/L
AV-001A	1,230	442.8
AV-002A	790	284.4
AV-003A	860	309.6
AV-005A	1,070	385.2
AV-006A	1,430	514.8
AV-007A	1,078	388.1
AV-008A	903	325.1
AV-009A	1,055	379.8
AV-011A	1,210	435.6
AV-027A	1,370	493.2

Table 1.

The National Academy of Science Report,15 Sep,1998,radon is a serious threat concluded,and USEPA approved ,a standard of 300 pCi/L in drinking water. Promulgation by USEPA has yet to occur while radon continues to cause lung cancer..The half life of radon is 3.825 days in which the radon level in every Wellhead blend in Table 1. would be reduce less than 300pCi/l.
A specific time for decay of radon to 300pCi/l can be determined by:

$$300pCi/L = (blend\ pCi/L)\ e^{-(3.825\ days)t}$$
where t is time to decay to 300pCi/L

A TDS standard of 500 mg/L is suggested as a standard for Tucson and, for sustainability, rendered legal and enforceable in a City Code.

Necessary radon decay times may be obtained, where possible, with stagnation times contingent upon chemical and physical parameters synchronized by the expertise available within the Tucson Water Department . The communications with personnel of the Tucson Water Department,particularly Mr Mohsen Belyani, Environmental Scientist, were exceptional.
The local mines say that they could possibly use Cap water, but its quality is not stable

The local mines say that they could possibly use Cap water, but its quality is not stable and its flow might be interrupted by a failure or routine maintenance of the Cap Canal(Ref: ag.Arizona.edu/SWES/tucwater2/resrsum.html). Does any one in Tucson have facts to negate the conclusions of the local mines?CAP cites repairs to canal are forthcoming, Colorado River floods and droughts are a certainty,addition of pollutants to Colorado River water are beyond the control of AZDEQ and local government entities. The deposition of salts, both municipally and privately on lots from gray water, are the antitheses of sustainability for Tucson and its citizens. Preparing for worst case scenarios can alleviate their effects if the plans include detailed facts and supporting calculations.A baseline of radioactive contaminants in CAP water is needed as a cleanup boundry condition in case Moab uranium reaches Tucson due to severe flooding. Sustaining the citizens of Tucson renders sustainability of Tucson.

Respectfully, *Clyde H. Stagner*
Clyde H Stagner, a citizen of Tucson

1 Inclosure:USGS email from Cheryl K Partin

cstampingr@dakotacom.net
_____

From:	"cstampingr@dakotacom.net" <cstamping@dakotacom.net>
To:	<Calkins.John@Azdeq.gov>
Sent:	Sunday, May 04, 2008 8:53 AM
Subject:	Fw: Arizona Daily Star Article

Dear Mr. Calkins,
  The publication cited may be of interest to ADEQ. In a worst case scenario:CAP water is contaminated with radioactivity as is the Phoenix watershed,sludge from sewage plants used for soil enhancement,and your facilities. In addition,with an evacuation of Phoenix SMA,PVNGS coolant effluent sources dry up and PVNGS electrical output would diminish and possibly cease.
  References are cited in text. For the citizens of Arizona,and my family, hopefully ADEQ has a disaster response plan,a recovery plan,and a long range productive plan.
  This email is open to any,and all,that may benefit from its content.
  Sincerely,Clyde H Stagner, a tax paying citizen of Tucson

cstampingr@dakotacom.net
_____

From:	"cstampingr@dakotacom.net" <cstamping@dakotacom.net>
To:	"Brian Henning" <bhenning@cap-az.com>
Sent:	Wednesday, June 11, 2008 6:58 AM
Subject:	Recharge Water Quality

Dear Mr. Henning,
  In accordance with the provisions of the CAP 2007 Water Quality Annual Report, request the public record of quarterly monitoring quality reports for the Avra Valley Recharge Project,Lower Santa Cruz Recharge Project. and the Pima Mine Road Recharge Project as required by the permitting process for regulatory compliance.
  Sincerely,Clyde H Stagner,citizen of Tucson

RDB file created by NWIS qwflatout program on sun0daztcn at 12/06/2007 16:55:26		
STAID Station number		
SNAME Station name		
DATES Date as yyyymmdd		
TIMES Sample start time		
LATLG Latitude-longitude		
P00061 Discharge, instantaneous, cubic feet per second		
P09510 Alpha-emitting isotopes of radium, water, filtered, planchet count, picocuries per liter		
P80030 Gross alpha radioactivity, water, filtered, natural uranium curve, micrograms per liter		
P03515 Gross beta radioactivity, water, filtered, Cs-137 curve, picocuries per liter		
P80050 Gross beta radioactivity, water, filtered, Sr-90/Y-90 curve, picocuries per liter		
P82068 Potassium-40, water, filtered, picocuries per liter		
P22703 Uranium (natural), water, filtered, micrograms per liter		
P80040 Gross alpha radioactivity, suspended sediment, natural uranium curve, micrograms per liter		
P03516 Gross beta radioactivity, suspended sediment, Cs-137 curve, picocuries per liter		
P80060 Gross beta radioactivity, suspended sediment, Sr-90/Y-90 curve, picocuries per liter		

STAID	SNAME	DATES
09423000	COLORADO RIVER BELOW DAVIS DAM, AZ-NV	Jan 5 1981
09423000	COLORADO RIVER BELOW DAVIS DAM, AZ-NV	Feb 2 1981
09423000	COLORADO RIVER BELOW DAVIS DAM, AZ-NV	Mar 2 1981
09423000	COLORADO RIVER BELOW DAVIS DAM, AZ-NV	Apr 1 1981
09423000	COLORADO RIVER BELOW DAVIS DAM, AZ-NV	May 1 1981
09423000	COLORADO RIVER BELOW DAVIS DAM, AZ-NV	Jun 2 1981
09423000	COLORADO RIVER BELOW DAVIS DAM, AZ-NV	Jul 1 1981
09424000	COLORADO RIVER NR TOPOCK, AZ.	Jan 9 1981
09424000	COLORADO RIVER NR TOPOCK, AZ.	Feb 5 1981
09424000	COLORADO RIVER NR TOPOCK, AZ.	Mar 10 1981
09424000	COLORADO RIVER NR TOPOCK, AZ.	Apr 21 1981
09424000	COLORADO RIVER NR TOPOCK, AZ.	May 9 1981
09424000	COLORADO RIVER NR TOPOCK, AZ.	Jun 2 1981
09424000	COLORADO RIVER NR TOPOCK, AZ.	Jul 1 1981
09424000	COLORADO RIVER NR TOPOCK, AZ.	Aug 27 1981

TIMES	LAT	LONG	P00061	P09510	P80030	P03515	P80050	P82068
1400	351130	1143417	15300					3.5
1345	351130	1143417	5190					3.7
1400	351130	1143417	2090					3.3
1400	351130	1143417	18900					3.4
1530	351130	1143417	19300					3.5
1220	351130	1143417	18700					3.4
0900	351130	1143417	8520					3.7
1230	344115	1142743	10900					3.5
1145	344115	1142743	10700					4.0
1200	344115	1142743	10100					3.7
1230	344115	1142743	12100					3.4
1230	344115	1142743	10900					3.6
1000	344115	1142743	13700					3.6
1300	344115	1142743	13200					3.5
1030	344115	1142743	24000	.2	<5.5	4.6	3.5	

From: "cstampingr@dakotacom.net" <cstamping@dakotacom.net>
To: "Scott D. Egan" <Scott.Egan@pima.gov>
Sent: Monday, August 04, 2008 10:49 AM
Subject: Re: Graywater

Scott-the waste waters from Las Vegas and Henderson are returned to Lake Mead from which the Colorado River flows past Davis Dam and Toprock,Az to the CAP intake in the vicinity of Lake Havasu and thence to Tucson.
Tucson does not drink pure Las Vegas waste water but Tucson's CAP contains their waste water(diluted) and the Tucson Water CAP blend contains their waste water(further diluted).
Perchlorate monitoring results from Henderson can be found,"Perchlorate Monitoring Results Henderson to yhe lower--(Ref:ndep.NV.gov/BCA/file/perchlorate.
The CAP Canal Water Quality report for the San Xavier Pumping Plant 2006 cites a May monitoring result of 2.3 ug/L of Perchlorate. In Lake Mead female fish are becoming male due to perchlorate, etc.
--clyde

----- Original Message -----
From: Scott D. Egan
To: cstampingr@dakotacom.net
Sent: Monday, August 04, 2008 9:41 AM
Subject: RE: Graywater

Thank you for contacting the District 4 Office of Supervisor Ray Carroll. I will be sure that he sees your message as soon as possible. You have obviously done much research on this issue. There is one statement you made, however, which I do not believe is accurate: "The citizens of Tucson are drinking their waste water" which is not presently the case.
Thank you again,
Scott Egan
Executive Assistant to Ray Carroll
District 4

From: cstampingr@dakotacom.net [mailto:cstamping@dakotacom.net]
Sent: Sunday, August 03, 2008 12:09 PM
To: District4
Subject: Fw: Graywater

----- Original Message -----
From: cstampingr@dakotacom.net
To: mcweb@tucsonaz.gov
Sent: Sunday, August 03, 2008 11:39 AM
Subject: Graywater

Honorable Mayor and Council Members,
By the year 2025, and thereafter except for outstanding water credits, the annual withdrawal of water from an aquifer may not exceed the annual recharge. The annual natural recharge of the Tucson Basin is 66,000 acre-ft per year(Ref:Water Resources in the Tucson Basin,ag.arizona.edu/SWES/tucson).. Based on the 2000-2002 average annual storage increase of 35,000 acre-ft per year(Ref: Groundwater Users Advisory Council minutes, Tucson Active Management Area, Dec 7, 2004), the Avra Valley natural groundwater recharge is 17,500 acre-ft per year. The total possible available groundwater annually, based on 2008 water resources, is equal to:
66,000 acre-ft/yr + 17,500 acre-ft/yr = 83,500 acre-ft/yr
plus the CAP allotment of 135,000 acre-ft/yr(possibly 144,000 acre-ft/yr) gives a total of:
83,500 acre-ft/yr + 135,000 acre-ft/yr = 218,500 acre-ft/yr.
This is Tucson Water's total annual user available water total in acre-ft/yr (unless other water sources are obtained).Sustainability involves keeping the 218,500 acre/ft per year available for use.

28

Evaporation is the primary concern affecting the increase or decrease of the total cited,supra. Rainwater harvesting and collected water from air conditioning units can increase the total acre-ft/yr cited ,supra. Graywater reuse will reduce the total available acre-ft/yr.

Graywater is discharged only in areas where there is at least five feet between the point of discharge and the ground water table to protect ground water resources from possible contamination(Ref.Gray Water Irrigation Guide, Mar 19, 2003, nmenv.state.nm.US/OOTS/Gray%Water%20Irrigation%20Guide1). In 1971.on the Eckard College Campus,under the auspices of a Doctorate in Microbiology, funded by Florida Powwer Corporation, and witnessed by the undersigned, viable virus traveled through 14 feet of sloping earth in a period of two weeks (albeit their number was greatly reduced).

The proposed Tucson Graywater reuse Code endorses a possible maximum residential graywater production to Evapotranspiration which is:

Evapotranspiration=transpiration+evaporation

=flora leaf evaporation+ground evaporation

=total evaporation

=total residence graywater

which is a loss from the 218,500 acre-ft/yr

Should all new residential home owners avail themselves of Tucson`s graywater incentives, follow city employee graywater promotional efforts, and install graywater reuse systems, the loss of water is determined as follows:

Population served by Tucson Water in 2008 was 750,000(Ref: extrapolated from Fig. 2.3, 2008 Update to Water Plan:2000-2050,Tucson Water Dept.). Estimated Long Range Planning population to be served in 2030 is 1,405,799(Ref:Water Plan 2000-2050,Tucson Water. The increase in population between 2008 and 2030 is equal to 655,799. The average size family is three persons(Ref:Census 2000,Demographic Profile highlights) and

(655,799 persons)/(3 individuals/household)= 218,600 households

The amount of daily graywater per household equals 118 gal/household/day (Ref:Water Resources Availability for the Tucson Metropolitan Area,barbaralasky.com/tucson-water) and

(118 gal/household/day)x218,600 households=25,794,800 gal graywater/day and

25,794.800 gal/dayx365day/yr = 9415.102 million gal/yr and

(9415.102 million gal/yr)/(325,851 gal/acre-ft)=

28,890 acre-ft /yr loss of water to atmosphere.

Repeating the computations for Tucson Water Service Area long range planning population of 1,483,649 in 2050 results in a 32,320 acre-ft/yr loss of water which is 14.79 % of total available.

The total available water in 2025 of 218,500 acre-ft/yr is a constant: the graywater annual water loss is a variable related to the increase of residences installing graywater systems.

There are mitigating solutions other than plumbing involving responsibility and accountability. What scientific evidence does the City of Tucson/PimaCounty have for the avoidance of all known best method disinfection technology for wastewater prior to recharge which San Diego and Los Angeles are considering?

Las Vegas and Henderson,Nev are sending disinfected wastewater back into Lake Mead from whence it came. The citizens of Tucson are drinking their waste water. Thanks to Prop.200 and the citizens of Tucson,CAP water is recharged-no thanks to Tucson Water Dept.

Respecfully, Clyde H Stagner, a Tucson citizen

---

cstampingr@dakotacom.net

From: "cstampingr@dakotacom.net" <cstamping@dakotacom.net>
To: <bhenning@cap-az.com>
Sent: Saturday, November 24, 2007 12:18 PM
Subject: CAP

Dear Mr Henning,
In view of the tailing`s leaching from the Moab site into the Colorado River,why doesn`t Cap test its water for uranium and radon?
Sincerely
Clyde Stagner-Tucson

From:	"cstampingr@dakotacom.net" <cstamping@dakotacom.net>
To:	<info@tucsonpimawaterstudy.com>
Cc:	<mcweb@tucsonaz.gov>
Sent:	Saturday, September 06, 2008 10:16 AM
Subject:	Misinformation

Dear Water Study Members,

The US EPA defines contaminant as any physical, chemical, biological, or radiological substance or matter that has an adverse effect on air, water or soil(Ref:US EPA ,Terms of Environment:Glossary,Abbreviations,and Acronyms).

Your attention is invited to your Meeting Summary, June 11,2008, conducted in the Copper Room, Randolph Golf Course Club House, and in particular to Part 5 under History of Water and Wastewater in Tucson wherein Cris Avery responded and mentioned that contaminants in surface water are eliminated in the recharge process.

Some contaminants in the recharged CAP surface water, blended with the Avra Valley groundwater and serviced as potable water to Tucson citizens, are not eliminated in the recharge process.Total dissolved solids are not elimated. In addition, on July 8,2004 perchlorate monitoring results(Ref:AZDEQ:Perchlorates in Arizona):

WELL	PERCHLORATE, ppb
21 CAVSARP	2.4
22 CAVSARP	2.3
9 Avra Valley Recharge	2.4
2-P Avra Valley Recharge	2.4

and, on June 30, 2004, the Santa Cruz River downstream from the Roger Road Wastewater Treatment Plant had <4 ppb of perchlorate(Ref:AZDEQ:Perchlorates in Arizona).

Mr. Avery`s comment response(cited,supra) is not considered as intentionally misleading. This conclusion could be supported and verified by a Tucson Water Dept. corrective statement at the Tucson Pima Water Study water resources meeting(s) on Sept 10,or 17,2008.

The establishment of a Tucson Water Quality Department is indicated- preferably including Pima County Wastewater Management`s monitoring and labratory analysis requirements(onsite and offsite).

Respectfully,Clyde H Stagner,a Tucson and Pima County citizen

---

From: cstampingr@dakotacom.net [mailto:cstamping@dakotacom.net]
Sent: Friday, August 29, 2008 5:30 AM
To: District4
Subject: Fw: Tucson citizen equity for CAP Blend Drinking Water

Info-clyde
----- Original Message -----
From: cstampingr@dakotacom.net
To: info@tucsonpimawaterstudy.com
Cc: mcweb@tucsonaz.gov
Sent: Friday, August 29, 2008 5:14 AM
Subject: Tucson citizen equity for CAP Blend Drinking Water

29 Aug, 2008

Dear Study Group Members,

In the email letter entitled, "The Future of Perchlorate and Tucson," dated 8/25/08. the undersigned included in the monitoring data for perchlorate:Lake Mead water(1999),Tucson Water Dept. water (2001), CAVSARP water (2004), Avra Valley Recharge water (2004), Santa Cruz wastewater from Tucson(2004),and CAP water at the San Xavier Pumping Station(2006). This data confirms the conclusion for the flow of perchlorates from Lake Mead which includes the treated waste water from the Las Vegas metro area of southern Nevada.The presence of perchlorates in the Avra Valley Recharge Wells 9 and 2P in 2004 confirms the presence of Las Vegas waste water in the CAP-Avra Valley water blend distributed by the Tucson Water Dept.

For Tucson citizen equity,and my wife`s health, the undersigned respectfully requests a dimension scaled map (s) of the Tucson Water Department`s complete distribution piping network which delineates the piping distribution of the CAP-Avra Valley water blend in a single color, and the piping delineating the complete distribution of Tucson Groundwater in a single contrasting color.

The undersigned further requests that the map ,or each of the maps,delineating the piping, be certified and dated thereon by the signature of the Direcetor,City of Tucson Water Department.

Respectfully, Clyde H. Stagner,a Tucson citizen.

From:	"cstampingr@dakotacom.net" <cstamping@dakotacom.net>
To:	<info@tucsonpimawaterstudy.com>
Cc:	<mcweb@tucsonaz.gov>
Sent:	Friday, September 12, 2008 10:35 AM
Subject:	Pharmaceuticals in Drinking Water:ENVIRONMENTAL NEEDS

Dear Tucson Pima Water Study Members,   12 Sept 2008

Your attention is respectfully invited to the Arizona Daily Star,"At least 46 million exposed to meds in drinking water",Local Angle, Sept. 12,2008. The Tucson Water Dept`s response did not include the following:

US EPA states in its guidance(Ref:Federal Register, October 23, 2003,Volume 68, Number 205) that "watershed-based plans should address not only the sources of water quality impairment, but also any pollutants and sources of pollutants that need to be addressed to assure the long-term health of the watershed(sic,citizens of Tucson and Pima County), including both surface and groundwater that serve as sources of drinking water".The Pima Association of Governments(PAG) cites this reference in the endorsements and involvements by the Arizona Department of Environmental Quality(Ref:Watershed Approach to Water Quality Management Planning, pagnet.org/document/water/PC208/ch8_Apr06).THIS PARAGRAPH REQUIRES WATERSHED POLLUTANTS TO BE MONITORED IN ABSENCE OF A US EPA ESTABLISHED MCL STANDARD.

In 2005, the Govenor of Arizona appointed the Clean Colorado River Alliance to address Colorado River Water Quality. This Alliance selected the following pollutants of concern:

1. Nutrients(nitrogen,nitrates,ammonia,phosphorus)
2. Metals(chromium,uranium,copper,mercury,arsenic)
3. Endocrine disrupting compounds
4. Perchlorate
5. Bacteria/pathogens
6. Salinity/total dissolved solids
7. Sediment/turbidity

What has Tucson Water Dept. done about these pollutants? Is,THERE IS NO MCL , an answer? Is, AZDEQ`S RESPONSIBILITY,an answer when Tucson Water Dept. is responsible for the potable water for Tucson citizens. Advance weather monitoring is a necessity for hurricane prediction: medical tests provide preliminary warnings of disease,et al.

Perchlorate well monitoring data for Avra Valley CAP water recharrge(Ref: AZDEQ:Perchlorates in Arizona,2004)

WELL	PERCHLORATE,ppb
21 CAVSARP	2.4
22 CAVSARP	2.3
9 Avra Valley Recharge	2.4
2-P Avra valley Recharge	2.4

is factual data of Lake Mead`s(containing Las Vegas effluent) contaminant presence in Tucson Water Dept.`s groundwater-CAP blend potable water and contradictory to Chris Avery`s response,at the June 11,2008 Tucson Pima Water Study member meeting in the Copper Room, Randolph Golf Course Club House, that contaminants in surface water are eliminated in the recharge process. Monitoring measurements of Total Dissolved Solids are also contradictory.

There are three contaminants, Meprobamate(miltown),Diazepram(vallium), and Dilantin which could not be completely removed by treatment with UV 40 mJ, Chlorine 3.5 mg/L, and Ozone 2.5 mg/L at Las Vegas Wastewater Treatment facilities(Ref:Occurrence,Treatment, and Toxicological Relevance of EDC/PPCPs/clw.csiro.air/video_hmtl/2007/ Shane Snyder). The contents of this paragraph should not be considered as all inclusive as pertains to contaminants. Why doesn`t Tucson Water Dept monitor the Avra Valley Groundwater-Cap potable drinking water for these three contaminants? Does CAWCD`s Avra Valley CAP monitoring requirements(permitee) to Arizona Department of Water Resources(permitor) replace any monitoring deemed necessary by the Tucson Water Dept.?

The City Of Tucson needs an independant Water Quality Dept.

Respectfully,Clyde H. Stagner,a citizen of Tucson and Pima County

From:	"cstampingr@dakotacom.net" <cstamping@dakotacom.net>
To:	"Brian Henning" <bhenning@cap-az.com>
Sent:	Friday, June 20, 2008 4:21 PM
Subject:	Fw: Recharge Water Quality

Dear Mr.Henning,
 The2007 Cap Water Quality Report cited you as the contact-Stella Murillo has not responded to an email requesting the data information available to the public.
 Sincerely,Clyde H.Stagner,a Tucson citizen
----- Original Message -----
From:
To:
Sent: Wednesday, June 11, 2008 11:27 AM
Subject: Fw: Recharge Water Quality

Dear Stella Muurillo, You attention is invited to the email to Brian Henning. The cited water monitoring quality data forthe public is requested from you.
 Sincerely,Clyde H Stagner,a Tucson citizen
----- Original Message -----
From:
To:
Sent: Wednesday, June 11, 2008 10:41 AM
Subject: RE: Recharge Water Quality

From:	"cstampingr@dakotacom.net" <cstamping@dakotacom.net>
To:	<mcweb@tucsonaz.gov>
Sent:	Saturday, August 23, 2008 2:51 PM
Subject:	After quality,quantity sustainability

Dear Mayor and Council Members,
 Since state agencies are involved,this request is sent to the Mayor and Council instead of the applicable city entity.
 Under the provisions of Permit No. 71-564896.0001,CAP is required to estimate the daily evaporation (Ref:Permit Conditions;4,Monitoring Requirements;d,Operational Monitoring Requirements,ii-) from the wetted areas,in acres, within the Avra Valley Recharge Project for recharge basins:RB-1,RB-2,RB-3,and RB-4. Is this evaporative loss of water from these recharge basins debited to Tucson`s annual 144,000 Cap water allocation? If so,what was the total annual 2007 CAP reduction in acre-feet?
 For all Tucson Water Dept. supplied open water recharge basins/open water storage areas/recreational ponds,lakes/other ,what is the total water evaporation in acre-feet from their wetted surfaces, individually identified, as specified in,"Evaporation from Open Water Surfaces ,in Arizona, by Keiyh R. Cooley,1970 (Ref:Permit No. 71-564896.0001, cited supra.
 From swimming pool surface areas determined from Pima County Health Dept. swimming pool permits, what is their annual loss of potable water,in acre feet, due to evaporation.
 What was the 2007 annual total wastewater effluent,in acre-feet, supplied to Commercial,Industrial,Government,and others.For each of the above identities,what was the total estimated evaporative loss in annul acre-feet? If the total acre-feet supplied does not equal the total evaporative loss, what was the disposition of the difference in quantities?
 This information is essential for water sustainability debits and credits.
 Respectfully,Clyde H. Stagner,a Tucson citizen

CHAPTER 4

TOTAL DISSOLVED SOLIDS (TDS)

Phoenix has a million tons of salt from CAP surface water coming into the valley annually from CAP surface water- and staying (Ref: Steve Rossi. Planner, Phoenix). For new homes in Tucson, with graywater stubs and installed graywater systems, 1044.5 pounds of TDS salts will be deposited on the property annually which is 15.7 tons in thirty years. This deposition of salts includes a buildup of potassium 40, radioactive with a long half life. Is this sustainability of Tucson citizen`s health and property values?

The Tucson Basin Desalinization Project, Group 3, supervised by Dr. James Riley, University of Arizona, , starting on 29 September. 2005, described scientific methodologies for removing salts and sustaining a potable water concentration of 450 TDS. The Tucson City Council has yet to act on the conclusions of Group 3.

The April 2008 Tucson Water Quality Report cited a 412 mg/L of TDS for Water Quality Zone 6 (WQZ6) . May 2008 maximum TDS mg/L concentrations of 585 (WQZ 1), 424 (WQZ 2), 464 (WQZ 3), 415 (WQZ 4), 426 (WQZ 5), 420 (WQZ 6), 412 (WQZ 7), 453 (WQZ 8), 536 (WQZ 9), and 419 (WQZ 10). The average range of TDS concentrations is statistically low compared to the maximum values experienced by individual recipients of Tucson water who suffer the TDS consequences because of where they reside in Tucson Water Department`s service area. The Pima Association of Governments (PAG) reported a 2001 reclaimed water (after blend) average TDS of 657 mg/L with Tucson Water Dept. cited as the source of the data.

Forty eight combinations of TDS treatment ,plant size, concentrate, and costs for disposal of TDS have been analyzed with recommendations for the City of Tucson in Report # 36, US Bureau of Reclamation. Four members of the Workgroup were Tucson Water Department personnel. The desalted product meets the City`s target levels of 210 mg/L TDS, 84 mg/L hardness, and 0.4 mg/L. The estimated costs for desalting range from a low of 0.1 cents/gal to a high of 0.124 cents/gal. One analysis cites a TDS pipeline to Yuma at a cost of $4000,850,000: another cites a TDS pipeline to Puerto Penasco at a cost of $300,770,000 (Ref: Reverse Osmosis Treatment of Central Arizona Project water for the City of Tucson, Tucson Water Department, Tucson, Az., USBR; Denver, Co., Jan 2004, Report #36).

The Tucson Water Plan 2000-2050, by the Tucson Water Dept., comprehensively analyzes water quantity for Tucson`s future and cites the need in 2006 for this decision, "What is the acceptable long-term mineral content target for the Clearwater Blended water program". The Tucson Water Dept recognized that the authority to render this decision rested elsewhere. The Tucson City Council did not render a decision by 2006 and has yet to render a decision.

Other than the TDS content, the Tucson Water Plan, 2000-2050, does not include Customer`s health sustainability- the plan is primarily quantity targeted.

From: "cstampingr@dakotacom.net" <cstamping@dakotacom.net>
To: <mcweb@tucsonaz.gov>
Sent: Wednesday, July 02, 2008 12:06 PM
Subject: Tucson water

Dear Honorable Mayor and Council Members,

The USEPA has designated for potable drinking water a Secondary Maximum Level for total dissolved solids (TDS) which is 500 mg/L. Noticable effects above Secondary Maximum Level include hardness,deposits,colored water,staining,and salty taste(Ref:USEPA,Ground Water and Drinking Water:Guidancce for Nuisance Chemicals,USEPA 8101 K-92-001). A high concentration of TDS will make drinking water impalatable (REF.USEPA, Monitoring and Assessing Water Quality,Nov 30,2006).

The 2006 CAP Water Quality sampling data cite an average concentration of 663 mg/L. At the San Xavier pumping plant in 2006, five of the 12 monthly consentrations of TDS were above 700 mg/L with a highest concentration of 726 mg/L.(Ref:CAP Canal Water Quality,Central Arizona Project,2006)

At the end of 2007,Tucson`s , Avra Valley drinking water source consisted of 45% CAP water and 55% native ground water. Tucson Water`s statement which followed affects the future of every Tucson citizen , "Over time, it will contain increasing percentage of recharged Colorado River water(Ref:Tucson Water 2007 CCR). Tucson Water has not been reined in by the Tucson City Council to a maximum TDS concentration in its potable drinking water. Tucson Water in its monthly pamphlet(with bill),Your Water Connection, cites a minimum TDS(Zone 7) of 302 mg/L and a maximum TDS of 439 mg?L(Zone 2).

Under the provisions of the Arizona Administrative Code: R 18-11-108 A. Surface water shall be free from pollutants in amounts or combinations that: 3.Cause oo-taste or oder in drinking water. A position that R 18-11-108 does not apply to blended CAP water is offset by the argument that the State of Arizona has enacted a precedent in regulation for "off-taste or odor" in drinking water. In other words, does the State of Arizona stipulate that surface drinking water shall be free from pollutants in amounts or combinations that cause off-taste or odor whereas off-taste or odor in ground water is acceptable for drinking?

Water safety and water quality reports from Phoenix to its citizens included incorrect or misleading data-or emitted it entirely(Ref:National Resources Defense Council www.tapintoquality.com/home). Phoenix Water`s CCRs for drinking water cited the following:

Year	Maximum TDS,mg/L
2002	856
2003	872
2004	702
2005	666
2006	812
2007	770

Salt water reduces life of household appliances such as a water heater, evaporative cooler, faucets,garbage disposal,dishwasher and clothes washer(Ref:Phoenix.gov,Phoenix Cass background,phoenix.gov/water/cassback). In 1997,the Colorado River water brought 1.1 million tons of salts with the estimated 1.4 million acre feet of CAP water imported into Central Arizona(Ref:Where do the salts go,waterresources.com/Documents 223). For Tucson Water`s annual CAP water import of 148,420 acre feet, a total of 116,616 tons of salts would accompany the water into Tucson.

Designation of maximum allowable concentrations of TDS, in public drinking water, is the responsibility of elected authorities. Since the State of Arizona has not acted,the responsibility lies with the Tucson City Council ,to designate by city code, a maximum allowable concentration of TDS in the potable water processed by the Tucson Water Department.

Such action provides boundry conditions for future operations,planning,infrstructure, and costs to both Tucson Water and the Pima Waste Water Management.

Respectfully,Clyde H Stagner,a Tucson citizen

34

From:	"cstampingr@dakotacom.net" <cstamping@dakotacom.net>
To:	<Moshen.Belyani@Tucsonaz.gov>
Sent:	Wednesday, May 28, 2008 11:14 AM
Subject:	TSW Water Plan 2000-2050

Dear Mr. Belyani
 Your attention is invited to TWS Water Plan 2000-2050:Critical Decisions page ES-7 which stipu
critical resource management decisions which must be made regarding the use of Colorado Rive
 Decision #1:What is an acceptable long-term mineral content target for the Clearwater blende
program.
Which also stated :Decisions #1 and #2 must be made by 2016
 The present Tucson-Pima Water Study group may/may not cite in the future, an answer to the q
oted supra in the interim the Tucson Water System is responsible for determing the answer to D
 Accordingly , what was the mg/L acceptable long term mineral content target for the Clearwater
program?
 As a part of the TWS outreach program has the mg/L target been disseminated to the public an
Southern Arizona Restaurant Association?
 Sincerely,clyde h stagner resident and taxpayer of Tucson

From:	"cstampingr@dakotacom.net" <cstamping@dakotacom.net>
To:	"Mohsen Belyani" <Mohsen.Belyani@tucsonaz.gov>
Sent:	Monday, May 26, 2008 8:32 AM
Subject:	Re:Water Concerns

Dear Mr.Belyani,
  As concerns CAP potable drinking water for Tucson, Tucson Water`s 2007
Annual Water Quality Report fails to cite Total Disolved Solids(TDS).Should
USEPA prohibit TWS from including TDS in the CCR,TWS could have inserted an
inclosure addressing the forthcoming paradox of increasing TDS in CAP
groundwater blend drinking water and the increasing TDS in groundwater due
to CAP. What is TWS`s projected maximum annual TDS for the next ten years
beginning with the year 2009 and resultant impacts physiologically and
household appliances.
  Concerning TWS citing in CCR`s no monitoring violations for 2007,your
attention is invited to SDWIS Violation Report,TUCSON
WATER-Catalina,Violation ID 1725,Violation ID 1709.compliance acheived with
date of response OCT-02-2007 renders the violation in effect earlier during
2007. Administrative and beaurocratic protocol may be mitigating but this
information is entered and displayed to the public as violations by TWS.
  In the TWS detailed information on Uranium, the use of "mildly" describing
its radioactivity is "mildly" deceiving.What human internal dose of uranium
is mild ?
  Sincerely,clyde h stagner,a Tucson citizen
----- Original Message -----
From: "Mohsen Belyani" <   >
To: "   " <   >
Cc: <   >; "Jeff Biggs" <   >; "John
Kmiec" <   >; "Martha Vanwinkle"
<   >; "Mitch Basefsky"
<   >
Sent: Monday, December 10, 2007 5:45 AM
Subject: Re: Radon Concerns

35

From: "cstampingr@dakotacom.net" <cstamping@dakotacom.net>
To: <mcweb@tucsonaz.gov>
Sent: Wednesday, June 18, 2008 1:55 AM
Subject: Tucson and CAP

Dear Honorable Mayor and Council Members,

  A letter document,dated 18 June,2008,titled as above,has been forwarded to the Tucson City Clerk for distribution to you.

  Cap water quality is discussed to include the effects of population growth,floods,droughts,CAP repairs,effects of concentrations on blends,residuals of nuclear testing-all of which support the local mines in their decision to continue their use of ground water for processing ore.

  One justification is included for a Tucson City Code citing 500mg/L as the standard for Total Disolved Solids (TDS). Presently, there is no boundry between Tucson Water`s existing TDS in water and an infinite TDS in Tucson`s potable water.

  Also included is a methodology for attaining the USEPA 300 pCi/l of radon in drinking water.

  Respectfully,Clyde H. Stagner,a citizen of Tucson

CHAPTER 5

PERCHLORATES

Perchlorates are salts occurring both naturally and by manufacturing for medical use and solid rocket fuel among others. Most per chlorate salts are soluble in water with difficulty to remove there from. The percholates from the Las Vegas Wash via the CAP canal to Tucson are not removed during recharge into ground water at Avra Valley and remain in the Clearwater blend of CAP surface water-Avra Valley groundwater distributed by the Tucson Water Dept in its service area. Subsequently, after passing physiologically through Tucson residents, the per chlorates reappear in the Pima County wastewater effluent discharged into the Santa Cruz River. Perchlorates in an end spatial/terrestial environmental enclosure will remain therein and continue to recycle over time.

Perchlorates have adverse health effects on infants and adults depending on the dose received. The USEPA has issued a reference dose (RfD) of 0.7 ug/L which does not require mandatory compliance. The Food and Drug Administration has developed a methodology for computing the perchlorate dose received from contaminated foods irrigated with contaminated water. The total human dose is the sum of the food dose plus the potable water dose.

The Tucson Water Dept., in its 2001 Annual Quality Report listed a monitoring measured range of <4-11.9 ppb for per chlorates. Subsequent Annual Water Quality Reports do not list any monitoring results for per chlorates . The Arizona Dept. of Health established an advisory health based guidance level (HBGL) whereas California` s level is 6ppb and Massachusetts ` is 2 ppb. The USEPA, in September 2008, decided to forego establishing an MCL for per chlorates - an MCL is expected in 2009.

From: "cstampingr@dakotacom.net" <cstamping@dakotacom.net>
To: <MitchBasefsky@Tucsonaz.gov>
Sent: Monday, August 18, 2008 7:14 AM
Subject: Fw: Tucson HABOOB:Perchlorate

info-clyde
----- Original Message -----
From: cstampingr@dakotacom.net
To: info@tucsonpimawaterstudy.com
Cc: mcweb@tucsonaz.gov
Sent: Monday, August 18, 2008 6:54 AM
Subject: Tucson HABOOB:Perchlorate

Dear Study Members,
  1. Tucson Health Considerations:
     The USEPA has not designated an MCL for perchlorate(Ref:Tucson Water Dept.,Mitch Basefsky).The USEPA is in the process of assessment for a drinking water perchlorate MCL. On 18,Feb, 2005, the USEPA issued a reference dose(RfD) for perchlorate which is 0.0007 mg/kg/day and a numerical estimate of a daily oral exposure based on body weight. The human population is not likely to experience harmful effects during a lifetime but it is a threshold for producing effects(Ref:USEPA Glossary). The RfD is not a mandatory compliance contaminant level. Voluntary compliance is indicated for drinking water:
     A. To protect the health of Tucson citizens consistant with the findings of the National Academy of Sciences (Ref: Groundwater and Drinking Water,USEPA:Final Chemical Spill-19,Groundwater Plume Interim,Record of Decisions,Apr,2006, Section 2.10.2).
     B. To avoid lawsuits similar to that filed in California because of Colorado River Perchlorate contamination (Ref:Groundwater Recharge,Perchlorate and the Colorado River.The estimate limit of quantification(LOQ) is 0.5 ppb for drinking water(Ref:Weitz and Luxenberg,PC,lawyer advertisement on the internet).
     The drinking water equivalent of the RfD of 0.0007 mg/kg/day is 24.5 ppb based on one human body weight of 70 kg and 2 liters of drinking water consumed per day(Ref:Testimony,Benjamin H. Grumbles,USEPA,May 6,2008)
     The dose of perchlorate to infants varies from that of adults. For example,in general, infants need daily drinking water equal to 150ml/kg of body weight(Ref:NIH,Human Water Consumption). An infant weighing 10 kg needs 1500ml daily:

    10 kg x 0.7 ug/kg/day = 7 ug/day
and (7 ug/day) / (1.5 L/day = 4.67 ug/L
which is the maximum perchlorate concentration in drinking water for this infant to avoid exceeding the consumption of the RfD of 0.7 ug/kg/day.
     Foods with higher content of water ,such as produce,would be expected to contain higher levels of perchlorate, a highly soluble chemical,and contribute more to the overall dietary exposure to perchlorate than food with lower water content.The results of this assessment do not represent the total human exposure to perchlorate (Ref:Preliminary Estimate of Perchlorate Dietary Exposure Based on FDA 2004/2005 Exploritory Data,US Food and Drug Administration, May, 2007). When the average child consumes perchlorate contaminated drinking water either alone or with perchlorate contaminated food,the amount of ingested perchlorate has the potential to exceed nearly every one of the proposed final drinking water standards, except the Massachusetts standard of 2ppb,thereby subjecting them to the adverse health effects of perchlorate(Ref:FDA Reports Perchlorate Widespread,Millions of Children at Risk from Exposure Levels, US House of Representatives, US Committee on Energy and Commerce, Jan.22,2008).
  Examples of Perchlorate Total concentration for food and drinking water on the same day are:
  B. Tucson Water Dept. maximum concentration of 11.9 ppb cited in 2001 Annual Quality Water Report:

Age (yrs)	Wt (kg)	Food** (ug/kg)	Drinking water (L) (UG) (ug/kg)	DailyTotal (ug/kg)
6-11mo*	9.4	0.29	1.4 16.7 1.77	2.06
6	23	0.28	0.748 8.9 0.387	0.774
25<35	64.6	0.11	2.10 5.67 .0877	0.198

*In general,infants need 150mL water/kg body weight-a person needs 1/2 ounce of water for each lb of body weight(Ref:NIH Human Water Consumption:Mayo Clinic,Wellness and Water Intake).
**US Food and Drug Administration Total Diet Study,Journal of Exposure,Science,andEnvironmental

Epidemiology,2008.1-10).

Table 1

C. Las Vegas:SNWS-River Mountains Smith Water Treatment Plant 2008 Water Quality Summary:Perchlorate Average Value of 3ppb:

Age (yr)	Drinking Water			Total daily Intake
	(L)	(UG)	(ug/kg)	(ug/kg)
6-11mo	1.4	4.2	0.447	0.737***
6	0.748	1.79	0.078	0.358
25<35 female	2.1	6.3	0.098	0.208

***Exceeds RfD

Table 2.

2.Sources of Perchlorate:

In May,1999,ADEQ monitoring showed 11ppb of perchlorate throughout Arizona(Ref:ADEQ).Latest results from Willow Beach,Az.,show levels of perchlorate in the 4ppb range(Ref:ADEQ) The primary sources of the perchlorate are the two locations of abandoned perchlorate production for rocket fuel located in the vicinity of Las Vegas,Nev. Perchlorate travels from these locations to the Las Vegas Wash,thence to Lake Mead,thence down stream in the lower Colorado River before entering the CAP canal and traveling to Tucson.The Lower Colorado River, which stretches from Lake Mead to the Mexican border,had measurable concentrations of perchlorate over its entire length(Ref:Perchlorate Treatment technology Update,EPA542-R-05-015,May,2005. In 2000,the perchlorate concentration, at the Las Vegas drinking water intale from Lake Mead,averaged 24ppb (Ref:Automated System Measures Flow Direction,Velocity in Wells,USGS).

The State of Arizona has an advisory level of 14ppb-1998 health based guidance level to be reviewed after EPA issues final RfD-which EPA did in Feb,2005.

3. Perchlorate Treatment and Removal:

Perchlorate clean up is in progress adjacent to Las Vegas. The drinking water cleanup level range established by USEPA is 4ug/L to 18 ug/L(Ref:Section 111.12 Ground Water Cleanup Levels;Section IV-1.2) Hoover Dam concentration in 2005 was 4ppb and < or = 4ppb at the Colorado River Aquaduct:California entry for Colorado River ater and near Colorado River water entry to CAP canal(Ref:Clean Colorado River Alliance:Recomendations to address Colorado River Quality,2006).

Once dissolved,the perchlorate anion is extremely mobile and very stable,requiring decades to naturally degrade and can have advection flow. The use of conventional water treatment technologies has proven to be largely ineffective for perchlorate removal because of its low reactivity,low volitility,and high solubility (Urbansky,1999).Perchlorate is very chemically stable under normal groundwater and surface water conditions (Urbansky,1999). Under these conditions,the recharge of perchlorate contaminated water results in similar perchlorate contaminated water upon withdrawal from the aquifer.

Ex situ biological treatment of perchlorate includes selection of appropriate electron donor and bioreactor configuration:the State of Califonia Dept. of Health Services has accepted the use of biological treatment to remove,or reduce, perchlorate from source water that might be used as a potable water supply(DHS,2002).The reference for this paragraph is:Final,Perchlorate Treatment Technologies Literature Review Overall Unit 1 Expend Treatability Study;National Aeronautics and Space Administration,Jet Propulsion Labratory.Pasedena,Ca,EPA ID# CA9800013030).

CAP water at the Mark Wilmer Pumping Plant.Parker,Az, had a May,2006,perchlorate level of 2.1 ug/L. The San Xavier Pumping Plant had a May,2006. level of 2.3 ug/L of perchlorate.The levels of perchlorate in CAP water vary with with the seasons,Colorado River Flow,and water levels in Lake Mead.

3.Conclusions:

A. Perchlorate is flowing into Tucson drinking water via the CAP water recharge blend at Avra Valley.The Tucson Water Dept`s remediation consists only of blending with Avra Valley groundwater. Tucson Water Dept. has stated that it will increase the % of Cap water in the blend which will increase the perchlorate level in Tucson drinking water.There are no available monitoring results by Tucson Water Dept. showing monitoring of the CAP water blend for perchlolate.

B. With a continuation of the discharge of 45 million gallons of effluent,as presently treated, into the Sata Cruz River,the Pima Waste Water Treatment Plant effluent flow shall eventually contaminate the AK-Chin reservation with perchlorates-an invasion.

C. In Tucson,the 2001 daily intake of perchlorate exceeds the RfD for infants and six year olds exceeds the USEPA RfD(Table 1.) The 2008 Las Vegas Water Quality Report percholate level causes the infant dose to exceed the USEPA RfD(Table 2.) The citizens of Tucson are drinking diluted waste water from Las Vegas,Nevada.

D. An independant Tucson Water Quality Department(or a Tucson/Pima Water Quality Labratory) responsible for drinking water(and waste water) monitoring,sampling, measuring,reporting,publishing,analysis,and assessment separated from the quantity operator is indicated.How many other stable chemical contaminants are traveling the water recharge route? Las Vegas water treatment plants are monitoring pharmaceuticals and endrocrine contaminants-will any of these disrupt biomass treatment?

Due to testosterone from Las Vegas ,male fish in Lake Mead are becoming effiminant? Shall this happen in Tucson?

Repectfully,Clyde H Stagner,a Tucson citizen

cstampingr@dakotacom.net

From: "cstampingr@dakotacom.net" <cstamping@dakotacom.net>
To: <mcweb@tucsonaz.gov>
Sent: Saturday, September 06, 2008 10:31 AM
Subject: Fw: Misinformation

info-clyde
----- Original Message -----
From:
To:
Cc:
Sent: Saturday, September 06, 2008 10:16 AM
Subject: Misinformation

Dear Water Study Members,

The US EPA defines contaminant as any physical, chemical, biological, or radiological substance or matter that has an adverse effect on air, water or soil(Ref:US EPA ,Terms of Environment:Glossary,Abbreviations,and Acronyms).

Your attention is invited to your Meeting Summary, June 11,2008, conducted in the Copper Room, Randolph Golf Course Club House, and in particular to Part 5 under History of Water and Wastewater in Tucson wherein Cris Avery responded and mentioned that contaminants in surface water are eliminated in the recharge process.

Some contaminants in the recharged CAP surface water, blended with the Avra Valley groundwater and serviced as potable water to Tucson citizens, are not eliminated in the recharge process.Total dissolved solids are not elimated. In addition, on July 8,2004 perchlorate monitoring results(Ref:AZDEQ:Perchlorates in Arizona):

WELL	PERCHLORATE, ppb
21 CAVSARP	2.4
22 CAVSARP	2.3
9 Avra Valley Recharge	2.4
2-P Avra Valley Recharge	2.4

and, on June 30, 2004, the Santa Cruz River downstream from the Roger Road Wastewater Treatment Plant had <4 ppb of perchlorate(Ref:AZDEQ:Perchlorates in Arizona).

Mr. Avery`s comment response(cited,supra) is not considered as intentionally misleading. This conclusion could be supported and verified by a Tucson Water Dept. corrective statement at the Tucson Pima Water Study water resources meeting(s) on Sept 10,or 17,2008.

The establishment of a Tucson Water Quality Department is indicated- preferably including Pima County Wastewater Management`s monitoring and labratory analysis requirements(onsite and offsite).

Respectfully,Clyde H Stagner,a Tucson and Pima County citizen

From: "cstampingr@dakotacom.net" <cstamping@dakotacom.net>
To: <mcweb@tucsonaz.gov>
Sent: Thursday, August 07, 2008 5:59 PM
Subject: Re: Tucson Water & Perchlorates

----- Original Message -----
From: cstampingr@dakotacom.net
To: mcweb@tucsonaz.gov
Sent: Thursday, August 07, 2008 5:29 PM
Subject: Tucson Water & Perchlorates

Dear Honorable Mayor and Council Members,
   The Citizens of Tucson are drinking the diluted, contaminated waste water from Las Vegas and Henderson,Nevada. Delivery of drinking water from the Central Avra Valley Storage and Recovery Project began in 2001(Ref:Tucson Water: Central Avra Valley Storage and Recovery Project).
   The CAP Water Quality Report,2006, at the San Xavier Pumping Station cites a perchlorate contamination of 2.3 ug/L in May, 2006. Of greater signifigance is the City of Tucson's Water Department 2001 Annual Quality Report which cites measured perchlorate contamination of <4-11.9 ppb which equals a maximum of 11.9 ug/L. This Tucson Water's Quality Report cites the major source of this perchlorate as,"a primary ingredient of solid rocket propellant". Perchlorate monitoring results for Henderson, Nev., can be found in,"Perchlorate Monitoring Results Henderson to---(Ref:ndep.NV.gov/BCA/file/perchlorate).The perchlorate path is Las Vegas Wash to Las Vegas Bay to Lake Mead to Colorado River in Arizona to CAP canal to Tucson. Las Vegas Wash delivers tertiary treated waste water effluent, non potable shallow groundwater seepage ,and runoff from the urbanized Las Vegas Valley to Lake Mead(Ref:pubs.acs.org/cgi-bin/abstract).
   Large doses of perchlorate have been shown to inhibit iodine uptake and reduce thyroid hormone production which can contribute to metabolic problems in adults and abnormal neurodevelopment during gestation and infancy (Ref:Thyroid Alert:Low Iodine and Perchlorate Effects on Women,Richard Dahl,EHP Environmental Health,Dec, 2006 via NIH).
   Perchlorate was placed on the Unregulated Contaminant Monitoring Rule(UCMR),1999, List 1,assessment monitoring with the method(sic, measurement protocol) listed as reserved(Ref:UCMR for Public Water Systems,Federal Register Environmental Documents,Mar 2,2000,USEPA). All large community water systems servicing more than 10,000 persons were required to monitor for perchlorates under the revised UCMR with the monitoring period from Jan 1,2001-Dec31,2003. Tucson Water's 2001 monitoring result is cited,supra. The Tucson Water Dept was cited for failure to monitor Alachor(perchlorate) in USEPA ID 114202. Compliance was finally acheived on Mar 29, 2004 an Dec 06,2006. Does this several years delayed monitoring compliance by the Tucson Water Dept represent responsibility and accountability for the pregnant women and babies of Tucson? Does the delay represent avoidance of reporting to USEPA another high concentration of perchlorate in Tucson water ? Why were'nt the monitoring results of the compliance made public?
   The USEPA established an MCLG of zero for perchlorate and an MCL = 2ug/L for perchlorate With Tucson Water Dept.'s measured concentration of 11.9 ug/L(exceeds MCL) and CAP's Water Quality measurement of 2.3 ug/L(exceeds MCL) of perchlorate at San Xavier Pumping Station, why isn't Tucson Water monitoring tucson's drinking water for perchlorates and making the citizens of Tucson publicly aware of the results.
   Also of critical importance to the citizens of Tucson is the admission by the Tucson Water Dept. that:
   1. the citizens of Tucson are drinking diluted waste water from Las Vegas and Henderson, Nev,and
   2.The recharge of CAP water in Avra Valley is not successfully removing all contaminants nor decreasing all the contaminants to USEPA MCL standards which represents a risk to the populace.
   The elected members of the Tucson City Council are responsible and accountable.
   Respectfully,Clyde H Stagner. a Tucson citizen

From: "cstampingr@dakotacom.net" <cstamping@dakotacom.net>
To: <info@tucsonpimawaterstudy.com>
Sent: Monday, June 09, 2008 3:57 PM
Subject: Fw: "gray water"

water info=clyde h stagner
—— Original Message ——
From:
To:
Sent: Saturday, June 07, 2008 9:48 AM
Subject: "gray water"

Re:The 7 Jume, 2008, article,"Panel:New Homes should have drain pipes to outside".
Webster`s unabridged dictionary,2d Edution,Random House' 2000, cites the following for "sustain":
  bear the weight of
  bear a burden
  endure without yielding
  keep from giving away
  keep up or keep going
  to supply with necessities of life
  to provide for an institution by furnishing funds or means
  to support by aid or approval
  to uphold as valid,or correct,a claim
  to confirm or corroborate
  For each of the above citatations,ask this question:FOR WHOM?" An answer other than a citizen,or citizens of Tucson, such as real estate sales,newspaper subscriptions,retail sales,increased population,more government control and/authority
represent vested interests anticipating profit from growth.
  Concerning new home "gray water" plumbing-is there a favorable citizen consensus or shall the elected leaders of Tucson claim to know what the dictatorial best is for the disorganized citizens of Tucson.
  Concerning "gray water" plumbing. A T connection should be required whereby the citizen has choice for using,or sending to sewer, the gray water. This choice has applicability for body,and clothing, decontamination in case of radioactivity from an accident or terrorist activity- the alternative is deposition,and buildup, of radioactive contamination on the citizen`s property. In 1962,a subordinate in a helicopter flew into ground zero after the detonation of Small Boy at the Nevada Test Site—seven lenthy showers were necessary to acheive acceptable body radioactive decontamination. What is Tucson`s emergency specific response plan for such contaminated Tucson citizens?
  The present flow of gray water goes to Pima County Waste Management where it can be converted to irrigational effluent. Why deviate from this proven workable system and its infrastructure?
                    Clyde H. Stagner,
                    8565 Pembrook Drive,
                    Tucson, Az 85715
                    Retired:Instructor,Nuclear Weapons MOS 8 7330

42

From:	"cstampingr@dakotacom.net" <cstamping@dakotacom.net>
To:	<info@tucsonpimawaterstudy.com>
Cc:	<mcweb@tucson.gov>
Sent:	Monday, August 25, 2008 4:03 PM
Subject:	The Future of Perchlorate and Tucson

Dear Tucson Pima Water Study Members,

The Center for Disease Control(CDC) found perchlorate in the urine of every person tested(Ref:Organic Consumers Association). The US EPA has established a reference dose of 0.7 ug/L-an MCL for perchlorate may be designated by US EPA in 2008. FDA has designated perchlorate intake doses from food for different ages of US citizens. The perchlorate sum of daily oral water and food intake is the total daily human perchlorate dose.

Relative perchlorate history for Tucson:

1999: Lake Mead water in 1999 contained 480 ppb of perchlorate(Ref:ADEQ).

2000: Saddle Island in Lake Mead contained 9.87 ppb of perchlorate(ADEQ).

2001: Tucson Water Dept. reported a drinking water maximum of 11.9 ppb of perchlorate in its 2001 Annual Water Quality Report.

2004: On July 8, 2004,perchlorate monitoring results were(Ref:AZDEQ:Perchloate in Arizona)

	WELL	ppb
1.	21 CAVSARP	2.4
2.	22 CAVSARP	2.3
3.	9 Avra Valley Recharge	2.4
4.	2-P Avra Valley Recharge	2.4

2004: On June 30, 2004, the Santa Cruz River downstream from Roger Road Wastewater Treatment Plant had <4ppb of perchlorate(Ref:ADEQ).

NOTE:FLOW PATH OF PERCHLORATE IS: LAKE MEAD, LOWER COLORADO RIVER, CAP CANAL, AVRA VALLEY CAP WATER INTO TUCSON POTABLE WATER, THROUGH TUCSON CITIZENS INTO PIMA COUNTY WASTEWATER, INTO SANTA CRUZ RIVER. Tucson citizens intake additional perchlorates from food and beer.

2005: In 2005,Hoover Dam had 4 ppb of perchlorates(Ref: Clean Colorado River Alliance:Recomendations to address Colorado River Quality,2006).

2006: The CAP Water Quality Report,2006, at the San Xavier Pumping Station cited a perchlorate contamination of 2.3 ppb in May,2006.

2008: Las Vegas drinking water is treated at two plants. The Las Vegas 2008 Water Quality Summary cites a maximum of 4.9 ppb perchlorate in drinking water from the Alfred Merritt Smith Water Treatment Plant and a maximum of 5.9 ppb in the drinking water from the River Mountain Water Treatment Plant. Both treatment plants intake their water from Lake Mead and their tertiary treated wastewater flows back into Lake Mead(Ref:Southern Nevada Water Systems).

Perchlorate remediation adjacent to Las Vegas Wash included(Ref: General Properties of Emerging Contaminants,Southern Nevada Water Authority).

2001. Ion Exchange

2002. One Pass Ion Exchange

2004. Fluid Bed Reactor Biological   Treatment.

2006. Initial Phase of in situ Biological Treatment.

The multiple treatment processes indicate an exponential remediation,ie,each identical removing pass removes the same percentage of the contaminant existing prior to the pass.For example,break a loaf of bread in two,break each remaining half into halves-keep repeating the process which results in smaller and smaller pieces and less quantity per energy input. Final result:some bread(or contaminant) always remains.

The Tucson Water Dept is presently serving the citizens of Tucson diluted tertiary treated,recharged water from Las Vegas and Lake Mead via the lower Colorado River and CAP Canal. A sustainability of total annual input water to Tucson Water Dept. providing for growth must consider the ultimate fate of two contaminants:total dissolved solids(TDS) and perchlorate(pharmaceuticals and endocrine disrupters are bring evaluated). Both contaminants shall increase their concentrations with time unless wastewater is transported out of Tucson Water`s inventory. Sustainability must have a boundry; otherwise, a Pima County Wastewater Treatment Plant would have to be designed to process an infinite floe of wasrewater.For sustainability, a designation of a TDS standard by the Tucson City Council
Treatment Plant is needed to plan and build treatment facilities.

For the perchlorate contaminant, monthly monitoring of the Avra Valley blend is needed. CAP does not,and is not required by the Central Arizona Water Conservation District (CAWCD) to monitor perchlorate. The CAWCD requires CAP to have CAP water and the blend at Avra Valley to be monitored and the monitoring to be performed by a labratory licensed by the Arizona Department of Health Services(ADHS),Office of Labratory Licensure and Certification using ADHS approved methods. Note the accountability separation between operator (CAP) and monitor(labratory).

Monitoring for perchlorates,by a labratory defined ,supra, or a Tucson Water Quality Dept, is indicated for the Avra Valley blended water. Perchlorate monitoring data is needed to determine: 1.whether Tucson Water is within the US EPA Referense Dose of 0.7 ug/L.,and 2.design and treatment requirements for removal of perchlorates from tertiary treated,recharged,potable water from Pima County wastewater effluent.

For sustainability, the wastewater flow of 45,000,000 gal/day=60,626 acre feet into the Santa Cruz River is recharged for use by Tucson Water:

Annual Source	Acre-Ft
Avra Valley natural recharge	~17,500
Tucson Basin natural recharge	~66,000
CAP Water Allocation	144,000
Total Input	227,500
Less effluent into Santa Cruz River	0
Less evaporative losses	?
less other losses	?
Remainder:Total recycled*	?

*This remainder,if positive, is the water available for future residential,industrial,and commercial growth.

A continuation of the 45,000,000 gal/day into the Santa Cruz River would reduce the Total Input,supra, to 166,873 acre-ft. The use of gray water in the residence increase of 218,00 households between 2008 and 2030 would further decrease the 166,873 acre-ft to 137,983 acre-ft and significantly reduce the acre-ft possibly available for growth.

Decisions are needed, boundry conditions determined, plans made with flexibility for changes(additional water souces,et al), and citizen approval obtained.Cooperation between the City of Tucson and Pima County is essential- perhaps the time has come for joint study sessions with Pima County Supervisors, Tucson Mayor, and City Councilpersons in attendance.

Respectfully,Clyde H. Stagner,a Tucson citizen.

cstampingr@dakotacom.net

From: "cstampingr@dakotacom.net" <cstamping@dakotacom.net>
To: <dpittman@azbuilders.org>
Sent: Friday, August 29, 2008 8:59 AM
Subject: Fw: Tucson citizen equity for CAP Blend Drinking Water

info-clyde
----- Original Message -----
From:
To:
Cc:
Sent: Friday, August 29, 2008 5:14 AM
Subject: Tucson citizen equity for CAP Blend Drinking Water

29 Aug, 2008
Dear Study Group Members,

In the email letter entitled, "The Future of Perchlorate and Tucson," dated 8/25/08. the undersigned included in the monitoring data for perchlorate:Lake Mead water(1999),Tucson Water Dept. water (2001), CAVSARP water (2004), Avra Valley Recharge water (2004), Santa Cruz wastewater from Tucson(2004),and CAP water at the San Xavier Pumping Station(2006). This data confirms the conclusion for the flow of perchlorates from Lake Mead which includes the treated waste water from the Las Vegas metro area of southern Nevada.The presence of perchlorates in the Avra Valley Recharge Wells 9 and 2P in 2004 confirms the presence of Las Vegas waste water in the CAP-Avra Valley water blend distributed by the Tucson Water Dept.

For Tucson citizen equity,and my wife`s health, the undersigned respectfully requests a dimension scaled map (s) of the Tucson Water Department`s complete distribution piping network which delineates the piping distribution of the CAP-Avra Valley water blend in a single color, and the piping delineating the complete distribution of Tucson Groundwater in a single contrasting color.

The undersigned further requests that the map ,or each of the maps,delineating the piping, be certified and dated thereon by the signature of the Directer,City of Tucson Water Department.

Respectfully, Clyde H. Stagner,a Tucson citizen.

CHAPTER 6

RADIOACTIVITY

In `1999, the USEPA attempted to promulgate a Radon 222 MCL of 300 pCi/L for potable drinking water as recommended by the US National Academy of Science (NAS). NAS estimated that radon causes about 20,000 lung cancer deaths each year- even very small exposures can result in lung cancer: any amount is harmful (Ref: USEPA, Radon, Risk Assessment Fact Sheet). The mitigation approach of including the Radon 222 airborne concentration in the MCL resulted in an abandonment of the legislation. The possible exposure to the adverse human health effect from potable water intake is increased by the addition of airborne exposure. In areas where basements are omitted in residence construction , a thick plastic sheet laid before pouring the concrete foundation, is a simple mitigating process. The Tucson City Council has yet to act.

Concentrations, below the USEPA recommended 300 pCi/L of Radon 222, can be achieved by vented time delay in distribution of potable water or by blending with a lower concentration source. The Tucson Water Department (TWD) has yet to act. In preparation for the anticipated USEPA MCL in 2000, the TWD did extensive monitoring of its well fields and water sources- since then monitoring for radon has ceased

In 1981 and 1986, the USGS monitored the Colorado River below Davis Dam and Topock, Arizona-both locations are between Hoover Dam and the Havisu Intake of CAP Colorado River surface water. Alpha emitting isotopes of radium, gross alpha radioactivity, gross beta activity, radioactive Potassium 40, natural Uranium and gross alpha and beta in sediments were detected and measured. Subsequent monitoring for these contaminants by CAP , ADEQ, or the TWD for the CAP surface water delivered to Tucson remained to be observed- if existent. The TWD monitors and reports results of adjusted alpha concentrations and Uranium activity in its Annual Water Quality Report distributed to its customers.

Radioactive Potassium 40 has a half life of one billion years and emit' s a beta particle with lesser numbers of gamma radiation The total amount will build up and increase with time as the graywater salts are deposited on residential property.

8565 Pembrook Drive
Tucson ,Az 85715

29 November, 2007

Tel:520 298 9192

Honorable Supervisor Ann Day,
130 W Congess,
11th Floor,
Tucson, Az 85701

Dear Honorable Supervisor Day,

The 1996 Safe Drinking Water Act Amendments required the Environmental Protection Agency (EPA) to establish several new health based drinking water regulations, including a multiple media mitigation (MMM) approach to address the public health risks for radon. National Drinking Water Regulation: Radon 222 was published in the Federal Register, Nov 2, 1999 (Volume 64,Number 211). EPA proposed new regulations for radon were published in the Federal Register(Volume 64, 59246).

For large consumer water sources (CWS), the proposed compliance for systems serving more than 10,000 people, the maximum concentration level (MCL) was 300 picocuries per liter (300 pCi/L) if the state and local CWS did not develop a local MMM program for radon in drinking water and in the air. Monitoring requirements were included in the proposed regulations. The proposed regulation was never promulgated. Congresses mandate to the EPA has never been promulgated to this date. The State of Arizona ,Pima County, and the City of Tucson have not promulgated a radon standard for drinking water.

The Tucson Water System in its 2001 Consumer Confidence Report (CCR) listed the following maximum radon levels which were sampled in 2000 or 2001 for the Tucson Water System including its Isolated Water Systems:

Water System	pCi/l	People Served
Catalina	160	1200
Coronado de Tucson	1604	1600
Diamond Bell	864	500
Rancho De Sol Lindo	1033	2800
Silver Bell	404	~240
Thunderhead	356	100
Valley View	789	500
Police Fire	88	~25
Tucson	1420	Remaining populace of metropolitannTucson not on individual wells

46

The CCR`s contain the statement,"Test results indicate that when compared with other concentrations for radon in the water supply, Tucson has fairly typical concentrations for radon in the water supply: Tucson Water System does not inform its customers of the National Academy of Science (NSA) report (NSA Rport,15 Sep 1998,radon is a serious public threat) and EPA`s proposed regulatory standard of 300 pCi/L for radon in drinking water. The long lived ancestors of radon remain under the surface of Pima County.

The Tucson Water System,including the Isolated Systems , in its 2006 CCRs listed required radionuclide levels but did not list any sampling, testing, or measured levels of radon. Radon was not listed. The state and local jurisdictions are empowered to establish mandatory standards for radon but have failed to do so.

EPA, in2000, based the 300 pCi/L radon standard on the water ingestion to occur over the individual life expectancy of seventy years(Ref:epa.gov/radiation/rdbpubs.htm, Page VII-7 and EPA 815-F-00-013 Nov 2, 2000). Today the life expectancy is 77.9 and

$$MCL(2000) \times 70 \text{ years} = MCL(2007) \times 80 \text{ years}$$
$$MCL(2007) = 270 \text{ pCi/L}$$

Which should be the promulgated mandatory 2008 drinking water standard for radon.

The drinking water in Tucson,and elsewhere,should be as safe as modern science justifies and stipulates for my wife, my children, my grandchildren, and my great grandchildren to drink. Your effort ,requiring the Tucson Water System to adopt the the Congressional mandate of 1996 by establishing a radon drinking water standard of 270 pCi/L, is respectfully requested to promote the general welfare as engraved in the Preamble to the United States Constitution.

Sincerely,and respectfully,

Clyde H. Stagner

From: "cstampingr@dakotacom.net" <cstamping@dakotacom.net>
To: <mcweb@tucsonaz.gov>
Sent: Sunday, June 08, 2008 4:48 PM
Subject: Sustainable Water Quality

Dear Honorable Council Members,
  Water testing by Tucson Water Dept in 2000 resulted in:

Water System	Radon:pCi/L	2- 1/2 lives later
Coronado de Tucson	1604	401
Diamond Bell	864	216
Rancho De Sol Lindo	1033	258
Thunderhead	356	89
Valley View	703	197
Tucson	1420	355

The levels cited above were maximum levels measured-remaining wells measured equal,or less ,per liter. The recommended standard for drinking water,by the American Academy of Science and USEPA is 300 pCi/l. The half life of radon is 3.825 day Two half lives, or 7.05 days, results in the pCi/l shown in column three,above. Transit time from wellhead to user would consume more time and urther lessen the levels cited in column three above.

  For new developments(homeowners will protect their children) require venting underground potable water storage tanks capable of storing 115 GPD X 7days= 805 gallons for a Tucson Water Dept.'s previously measured 1600 pCi/L and adjustments made to lesser tank volumes for lesser measured radon levels. An alternative would be a larger tank,installed by the developer,for the entire development.

  Tucson Water Dept can further the effort,over time, by increasing the time for water flow with venting enroute to user

  This methodology would also make available local emergency water supplies in case of natural or manmade disasters.Its applicability for fire fighting is at the discretion of the given fire department.

  That USEPA does not have a standard for radon in drinking water does not relieve elected leaders from their responsibility protect their citizens from a recognized hazard to their health.

  Respectfully,Clyde H Stagner, a Tucson citizen

>>> "cstampingr@dakotacom.net" <cstamping@dakotacom.net> 11/30/2007 12:27 PM >>>

Dear Mr Belyani,
  The 1996 Safe Drinking Water Act Amendments required the Environmental the EPA to establish several new health based drinking water regulations to address the public health risks for radon(Federal Register,Vol 64,Number211 and Vol 64,59246).

  The National Acedemy of Science(NSA Report.15 Sep, 1998,radon is a serious public threat) and the EPA`s proposed regulatory standard of 300 pCi/L for drinking water proposed in references cited,supra, were not promulgated. Are you and the Tucson Water System proud that water with radon in excess of 300 pCi/L is being delivered to Tucson`s citizens who have names and are individuals in contradistinction to statistical numbers.

  As one example ,does the Tucson Water System know, or claim, that the drinking water content of 1604 pCi/L of radon delivered to the ~ 1600 people of the Isolated System Coronado de Tucson in 2001 is safer and medically better than the NSA and EPA. There are other similar examples.

  The State of Arizona and the City of Tucson are empowered by the federal government to promulgate drinking water standards. What has Tucson Water done to attain the 300 pCi/l standard for the people of Tucson.

  Further, the standard of 300 pCi/L in 2000is based on water consumption over a 70 year lifespan. The lifespan is now 77.9 year which dictates a radon water quality standard of 270 pCi/L...

  This perspective has been communicated in writing on this date to each Tucson Councilperson, the Mayor, and each Pima County Supervisor with a request for each of them to promote the general welfare as engraved in the Preamble to the Constitution of the U nited Staes.

Clyde H Stagner

Δ8

From: "cstampingr@dakotacom.net" <cstamping@dakotacom.net>
To: <ndavid@cox.net>
Sent: Tuesday, July 08, 2008 3:58 PM
Subject: Fw: Response to your questions about radioactivity in ColoradoRiver water

Colorado River Hazmat-clyde
----- Original Message -----
From: "   " <   >
To: "Mitch Basefsky" <   >
Sent: Tuesday, July 08, 2008 3:35 PM
Subject: Re: Response to your questions about radioactivity in ColoradoRiver water

> Dear Mr. Basefsky,
> The Tucson Water radioactive monitoring is ground water monitoring. Until
> Tucson Water specifically cites the radioactive contaminations by
> monitoring for the % CAP and % Avra Valley groundwater,repectively,or by
> deduction from monitoring data results, Tucson Water has yet to show
> factual knowledge of the radioactive contaminantsin CAP water. CAP`s 2006
> Water Quality Report cites no monitoring for radioactivity in CAP water.
> For USGS sites USGS 0942000 andUSGS 0942300,both below Hoover Dam,There
> are nine sample IDs listing radioactive contaminants in Colorado River
> water. Radioactive sediments were among those monitored . These monitoring
> sites are above CAP intake from Colorado River.
> The approach taken in the Guideline for controlling radiological hazards
> has two stages;I. initial screening for gross alpha and/or beta activity
> to determine whether the activity concentrations are below levels at which
> no further action is required:2. if the screening levels are
> exceeded,investigation of individual radionuclides and comparison with
> specific guideline levels((Ref:WHO Drinking Water Standards,2006) the US
> is a member of WHO.
> USEPA states in its guidance(Ref:Federal Register,OCT 23, 2003,Vol 68,no.
> 205)that "watershed based-plans should address not only the sources of
> water quality impairment,but also any pollutants and sources of pollutants
> that need to be addressed to assure the long-term health of the
> watershed,including both surface and groundwater that serve as sources of
> drinking water
> Suppliers of drinking water subject to the US Clean Water Act cannot use
> the designated MCL Standards as a boundry for accountability and
> responsibility-as the previous paragraph stipulates.
> The existing baseline of radionuclides, with concentrations, in the CAP
> water is an asset to recovery operations in case radioactivity from a
> PVNGS reactor accident or uranium from a flooded MOAB,Utah, reaches Pima
> County-.
> Should you have questions,please communicate-Respectfully,Clyde H
> Stagner,a Tucson citizen- Original Message -----

From:	"cstampingr@dakotacom.net" <cstamping@dakotacom.net>
To:	<calkins.john@azdeq.gov>
Sent:	Tuesday, November 20, 2007 4:09 PM
Subject:	radionuclides

Dear Mr Calkins,
   Tucson Water Sampled and measured radionuclides which showed radon levels above 600 pC/L and> 1000 pC/l. Their 2006 CCR does not list Radon,Ra226,228,or uranium. In view of EPA`s and NSA`s findings for 300 pC/l as the MCL for non participating CWS in radon MMM. Why hasn`t the state promulgated a mandatory water standard for radionuclides.

   Under the provisions of ARS 49-223, I, Clyde H Stagner, petition the Director of the Arizona Department of Environmental Quality to establish a drinking water standard for Radon for which no drinking water standard exists in Arizona(pusuant to section 49-224,Subsection D).

         Sincerely,
            Clyde H. Stagner,
            8565 Pembrook Drive,
            Tucson Arizona 85715

>>>>> "   " <   > 7/4/2008 12:53
>> PM >>>
>> Dear Mr Basefsky,
>> In Planetsave,Is The Colorado River Becoming Radioactive from
>> Upstream
>> Uranium Mines?.by Max Lindberg,published on June 25th, 2008, writes:
>> "Taking my query a bit further,some 500 miles,I spoke with Mitch
>> Basefsky,PIO for the Tucson Water District,and he assured me they are
>> monitoring the level of radiation in water coming into the area from
>> the
>> Colorado River via the Central Arizona Project. Basefsky said they have
>> not
>> seen a change in water radioactivity over the years,but remain
>> concerned
>> that eventually,if nothing is done to stem the release of radioactive
>> materials into the river,it will become a broblem here."
>> Mr. Basefsky,where did Tucson Water monitor the CAP for
>> radioactivity,
>> what radioactive contaminants were monitored,what were the
>> the radioactive contaminants monitored, where were the results of the
>> monitoring published and recorded for the Tucson City Council and
>> public to
>> see?
>> As you stated this could be a problem here.
>> Respectfully,Clyde H Stagner,a Tucson citizen

   From: cstampingr@dakotacom.net [mailto:cstamping@dakotacom.net]
   Sent: Saturday, November 24, 2007 12:18 PM
   To: Brian Henning
   Subject: CAP

   Dear Mr Henning,
      In view of the tailing`s leaching from the Moab site into the Colorado River,why doesn`t Cap test its water for uranium and radon?
         Sincerely
            Clyde Stagner-Tucson

50

CHAPTER 7

GRAYWATER and HARVESTING

Graywater is bathroom sink, bath, and shower water plus washing machine water. This non potable residue is piped outside residences and used for irrigating flora. The outside graywater system (~$5,000) is a modified septic tank system without the use of biological purifiers. Application of this system to residences is touted as "potable water" sustainability-which is not necessarily the case for "water" sustainability.

To achieve "water" sustainability, the quantity of graywater discharged outside the residence must equal the irrigation need of the planted flora- this quantity of water is lost from the water provider total inventory by evapotranspiration. Graywater quantities discharged outside the residence in excess of the flora irrigation need are also lost, unnecessarily, from the provider`s total water inventory by evapotranspiration which reduces the provider`s total available water inventory (potable plus non potable) and is negative "water" sustainability. The City of Tucson advocates, by code and policy, the use of residential graywater without the necessary specifications to preclude unnecessary wasteful evapotranspiration.

The Tucson City Council appointed stakeholders for preliminary evaluations of a city code requiring new construction of residences to contain interior graywater plumbing with stub outs (~$500.00). Homeowners associations, health experts, and mechanical engineers were omitted from the stakeholder representation. Promulgation of the city code has the potential of losing 32,570 acre-ft of water annually by evapotranspiration-22.6% of Tucson`s annual CAP surface water allocation of 144,000 acre-ft annually.

Harvesting rainwater by businesses for irrigation is also touted as a means of saving potable water. The discussion for graywater in the preceding paragraphs is applicable to rainwater harvesting. Collection of rainwater with subsequent discharge into the city`s sewage system supports total water sustainability including rainwater which otherwise would be subject to total evapotranspiration.

From: "cstampingr@dakotacom.net" <cstamping@dakotacom.net>
To: <info@tucsonpimawaterstudy.com>
Sent: Monday, June 16, 2008 9:45 AM
Subject: Fw: Gray water

---- Original Message ----
From:
To:
Sent: Monday, June 16, 2008 9:29 AM
Subject: Gray water

Dear Honorable Mayor and Council Members,
   Older homes generate 45 gallons of gray water a day- new homes generate 35 gallons per person per day (Ref: 2000 Tucson census cites 2.4 persons per household.
   For new homes:
   35 gal/day/person x 2.4 persons/household=84gal/day
   Tucson water`s selection of Total Dissolved Solids (TDS) is 450 mg/L(solvent salts).
   Converting gal to liters:3.7854 L/gal x 84 gal/day=318 L/day
   Total salts:318 L/day x 450 mg/L= 143088 mg/day
which is 1430.88 grams/day
   Converting to pounds:1430.88 g/day x 0.002g/day=2.86 lbs/day
which,for one year equals 1044.5 lbs.
   For 30 years(mortgage),gray water deposited salts, on a typical new home in Tucson, is 15.7 tons of salts
   Gray water is anti-tucson sustainability. An already alkaline home lot becomes more alkaline. The entire area becomes a flora killer ubless the flora thrives on salts.Salt increases rising due to CAP are here to stay unless collected and transported elsewhere.
   Every property owner,cited above, would have the right to go to the County Assessor and demand a property tax reduction due to degradation of property value caused by required use of gray water. What would be the effect on the tax base?
   Respectfully,Clyde H Stagner,a citizen of Tucson

From: "cstampingr@dakotacom.net" <cstamping@dakotacom.net>
To: <mcweb@tucsonaz.gov>
Sent: Wednesday, July 16, 2008 2:16 PM
Subject: whereas

Dear Honorable Mayor and Council members
   The following amendment is submitted to the "Residential Gray Water Ordnance" AND the "Use of Rainwater Harvesting and Storage Systems:
   Whereas the citizens of Tucson are also citizens of Pima County and;
   Whereas the City of Tucson provides potable water to citizens of Tucson and citizens of Pima County residing outside the city limits of tucson and;
   Whereas all citizens being provided potable water by the City of Tucson are entitled to equity:

   BE IT ORDAINED BY THE MAYOR AND THE COUNCIL OF THE CITY OF TUCSON AS FOLLOWS:
   SECTION 1. The promulgation of the Residential Gray Water Ordnance and Tucson Code Chapter 6,new Article X as Tucson City Codes is contingent upon the adoption of Tucson Code,Chapter 6, and new Article X ,as Pima County Ordnances by a majority of Pima County Supervisors.

   Respectfully,Clyde H. Stagner,a Tucson citizen

52

From: "cstampingr@dakotacom.net" <cstamping@dakotacom.net>
To: <info@tucsonpimawaterstudy.com>
Sent: Sunday, June 22, 2008 9:23 AM
Subject: Fw: save money,save water,save effluent

info-clyde
----- Original Message -----
From: cstampingr@dakotacom.net
To: mcweb@tucsonaz.gov
Sent: Sunday, June 22, 2008 9:07 AM
Subject: save money,save water,save effluent

Dear Honorable Mayor and Councilpersons,
   Newer toilets use 1.6 gal per flush. Residents of homes flush toilets an average of 5.04 times per person per day (Ref: Residential water use summary,Aquacraft com/Publications).Flushing results in the use of 8.064 gallons of potable water per day per person. For a Tucson Water area projected population increase of 500,000, the total additional flushing gallons equals 4,032,000 per day and annually equals 1471,680,000 gal/yr =4516.4 acrefeet/yr
   According to the 2000 US Census,Tucson had 2.42 persons per household which required 19.5 gal of toilet flushing water per household.In the same household, one 20 gal shower per day per person(Ref:University Unitarian Universalist Society) results in 48.4 gal/day.
   The total daily household water of 19.5 gal for toilet flushing can be obtained from the daily showering residual of 48.4 gal.This can be accomplished by including in new residential home construction a Bath/shower water recycling system which transports residual shower water from the shower drain to a holding tank for toilet flushing with necessary water volume controls. The following listed patents are applicable to this system:
   US Patent 3112467
   US Patent 4162218
   US Patent 5345655
   West German Patent 2336744
   West German Patent 3828528
This system should not be considered for retrofitting because of installation costs.
   The total residential water saved per month is: 19.5gal/household/day x 30 day/month = 585 gal/household/month = 4.773 ccf and monthly water cost is 4.773ccf x $1.23 = $5.87
   With an installed Bath/shower recycling system, the total household water use is 3570 gal/month -585 gal/month =2985 gal/month = 3.99ccf and monthly water cost is $4.91 for a monthly savings of 96 cents or $11.52 annually which,in thirty years,may ,or,may not amortize the system cost.
   In comparison to the gray water program, the Bath/shower recycling system saves the Tucson citizen homeowner, or renter, some money,saves the Tucson Water Dept. some water supply,and reduces the sewage water flow to the Pima Waste Water Managemet facilities.Sustainability of the Tucson citizen is Tucson sustainability .
   Respectfully,Clyde H Stagner,a Tucson Citizen

8565 Pembrook Drive
Tucson, Az 85715

14 July. 2008

TUCSON PIMA WATER STUDY
PO BOX 2344
TUCSON,AZ 85701

Graywater created per household per day in Tucson is equal to(Ref:The University of Arizona Cooperative Extension,Cochise County):

35 gal/day x # of family members=gal of graywater daily

The average family size in Tucson is 3.12(Ref:US Census Bureau,Census 2000,dated December 19,2004) and:

35 gal/day x 3.12 family members= 109.2 gal/day of graywater
= 413.4 Liters per day.

The Las Vegas Water Quality Report, based on 2007 data, cited 4.7 ppb as the drinking water average Uranium content. The USEPA MCL is 30 ppb for Uranium: the USEPA MCLG is zero. Las Vegas water intake is from Lake Mead and wastewater return is via the Las Vegas Wash to Lake Mead.

Henderson, Nevada, in its 2008 Water Quality Report cites an average 4.8 ppb Uranium in its drinking water which is obtained from, and wastewater returned to, Lake Mead.

The USGS, on Aug 27, 1986, at location 09424000 on the Colorado River near Toprock, Az , in sample ID P22703 cites a maximum Uranium level of 4.3ug/L ~4.3ppb. The later years data from Las Vegas and Henderson is used for an average Uranium concentration in CAP water.

From Lake Mead to Cap entry into Arizona, Colorado River water diffusion is limited to rainfall. A contamination of CAP water shall be considered 4.75 ppb(average of Las Vegas and Henderson levels) of Uranium until CAP and/or Tucson Water Dept monitor CAP water for Uranium and release results to the public.

Tucson Water Dept. `s 2006 Annual Water Quality Report cited drinking water Uranium content ranging from 0.5 to 5.1 pCi/L and in its 2007 Annual Water Quality Report cited 1.5 to 4.5.5 ppb. Based on the later report, an average drinking water Uranium concentration for Tucson water is computed to be 3.0 ppb.

For 2007, the average daily drinking water production from Avra Valley was 51.76 million gallons per day with a blend of 46.6 % CAP water(Ref:Tucson Water Dept.) and this blend concentration of Uranium is computed by:

46.6 L(4.75 ppb)+53.4L(3.0 ppb)=381.59 ppb/100L=3.8 ppb/L~0.0038 mg/L

$$= 0.0038 \text{ mg/L of uranium}$$
$$= 3.8 \text{ pCi/L}$$

Providing a blend of Avra Valley CAP drinking water to comply with the USEPA MCLG for Total Dissolved Solids(TDS) of 500 mg/L requires 64% Cap(663mg/L) and 36% Avra Valley groundwater(210mg/L):

64L(663mg/L)+36L(210mg/L)=499.92mg/L~500mg/L of TDS

The uranium content of this blend is determined by:

64 L(4.75 ppb) + 36L(3.0 ppb) = 412 ppb/100L = 4.12 ppb/L = 0.00412 ppm/L

$$= 0.00412 \text{ mg/L}$$
$$= 4.12 \text{ pCi/L}$$

And the daily deposition of graywater uranium on a residential lot is given by:

413.4 L graywater x 4.12 pCi/L uranium = 1703 pCi uranium deposited daily

$$= 621671 \text{ pCi uranium annually}$$
$$= 6216710 \text{ pCi uranium in ten years}$$

Of the three Uranium isotopes, approximately 99% is U238 with a half life of 4.47 billion years and which decays by emitting an alpha particle. An alpha particle can be absorbed(stopped) by a sheet of paper. This stopping inside the human body causes tissue damage as was experienced in the Polonium assasination in Great Britain.

The effects of very low level ionizing radiation are very difficult to study. They are well below the levels of normal background radiation that people receive from natural sources. In fact,conclusions about the effects of low levels of radiation come from what we learned about the effects of higher levels of radiation exposure. As a result,*there is no firm basis for settings a "safe" level of exposure above background*(Ref:USEPA Radiation Information).

Children have been known to eat dirt:children playing in a yard get dirty. No one in a household will know if their child brings radioactivity into the house. No one in the house will know if the child's bath removed all of the radioactivity. The parents trusted the Tucson Water Dept. Some lots have zero percolation:some lots overflow during rainfall with spreading from one lot to another(s).

In 1981 and 1986,the USGS at Sta.... Numbers 0942300 and 0942400 on the Colorado River below Davis Dam,Az-Nv, and at Top rock ,Az, sampled(ID P2068) the Colorado River fourteen times for Potassium 40 with an average result of 3.557 pCi/L. The half life of radioactive Potassium 40 is 1,248 billion years. Of the emissions 89% emit a 1.311 MEV beta particle; the remaining 11% emit a gamma with an energy of 1.46 MEV. Due to the lack of water diffusion and the long half life of Potassium 40, the concentration of 3.557 pCi/L will reach the Tucson water and

Cap recharge location in Avra Valley. The CAP 2006 Water Quality does not show monitoring results for Potassium 40.

The concentration of Potassium 40 gamma emitters is:

3.557 pCi/L x .11 = 0.39 pCi/L of Cap Potassium 40 gamma emissions

And for beta emissions:

3.557 pCi/L - 0.39pCi/L = 3.167 pCi/L of CAP Potassium 40 beta emissions

The 2004 Tucson Water's Major Quality Parameters Report cited an average of 2.2 mg/L of potassium of which 0.012 is radioactive Potassium 40:

2.2 mg/L x 0.012 = 0.0264 mg/L of Potassium 40
                 = 0.187 pci/L

of this radioactive Potassium 40, 11% decays by gamma emmision which is:

0.0264 mg/L x 0.11 = 0.0029 mg/L of Potassium 40 gamma emissions
                   = 0.021 pCi/L of Potassium 40 gamma emissions

The remaining 89% of Potassium 40 beta emissions is:

0.0264 mg/L x 0.89 = 0.0235 mg/L of Potassium 40 beta emissions
                   = 1.7 pCi/L of Potassium 40 beta emissions

The gamma emitter concentration of Potassium 40 in the 500 mg TDS blend of Avra Valley CAP is:

64L(0.39pCi/L) + 36L(0.021 pCi/L) = 25.72 pCi/100L= 0.2572 pCi/L

The beta emitter concentration of Potassium 40 in the 500 TDS blend of of Avra Valley CAP is:

64 L(3.167 pCi/L) + 36 L(1.7 pCi/L) = 263.9 pCi/100L = 2.64 pCi/L

The daily graywater Potassium 40 gamma deposition is:

413.4 L/day x 0.2572 pCi/L = 106.3 pCi per day
                           = 38,809 pCi per year
                           = 388,090 pCi per ten years

The Potassium gamma radiation easily penetrates air and low density construction materials . The daily number of gamma emissions will increase as the concentration increases with time.

The 1.311 beta particle emitted by Potassium 40 can penetrate gloves and clothing(Ref: Physics for Radiation Protection-Handbook). This energy beta particle will penetrate 4 meters(~13 feet) resulting in a 13 foot radius sphere of radiation exposure from point of deposition.

There are no recent monitoring reports for radon in Tucson water and none by either CAP or Tucson Water for CAP water. USGS sample ID P80040,at Toprock,Az, measured alpha radioactivity in suspended sediments at < 0.7 ug/L. Data on the radium content of bottom sediment collected in 1960 and 1961 throughout the Colorado River Basin is provided in "Colorado River Basin Radioactive Materials, OSTI ID-7215422". Radon derived from the diffusion of bottom sediments is an important component of the radon budget in surface water at Honan South, located in South Australia, but does not account for all the radon(Ref:iah.org.au.pdfs/white). Lack of current CAP water data for radioactive materials limits the scope of accountability for the Avra Valley Cap water blends.

Radon levels in 1999 for the Avra Valley wellheads was published by Tucson Water The average radon concentration of the 22 AV wellheads was 1100 pCi/l- much higher than the National Academy of Science and USEPA`s level of 300 pCi/L for drinking water. For the Avra Valley CAP blend for 500mg/L TDS, the radon concentration is computed as:

$$64L + 36L(1100pCi/L) = 39600 \ pCI/100L = 396 \ pCi/L$$

Due to the 3+ day half life, some radon in the drinking water will decay during transit from wellhead to tap Tucson Water has published no criteria to obtain decay. The remaider in potable water, after household use will be flushed outside to decay in graywater.

CAP Water Quality Report cites TDS as 663 mg/L and avra Valley records show 210 mg/L. The TDS of the 500Mg/L CAP blend is:

$$64L(663mg/L) + 36(210mg/L)= 49992mg/100L = 499.92 \ mg/l \sim 500 \ mg/L$$

with the amount of salts disposed in graywater equal to:

413.4 L graywater x 500mg/L = 206,700 mg daily= 206.7 grams daily
$$= 754455 \text{ grams yearly}$$
$$= 166 \text{ pounds annually}$$
$$= 1,660 \text{ pounds in ten years}$$

CAP Water Quality cites the benefits of Calcium and Magnesium in drinking water. For the Calcium to be nutrient available, Vitamin D must be added to drinking water which has not been done(Ref:Virginia Cooperative Extension, Virginia Tech).

Residential air born radon is included herein because of the environmental impacts of graywater- synergistic effects may,or may not, be applicable. The maximum air born concentration of radon in homes has been designated by USEPA as 4 pCi/L. In 1987/1988,an EPA/Arizona Radiation Regulatory Agency conducted a survey in Pima County to determine indoor radon concentrations with the following results:

ZIP CODE	# RESIDENCES	EXCEEDING 4pCi/L	HIGHEST pCi/L
85629	20	1	4.70
85641	8	-	-
85701	2	-	-
85704	27	-	-
85705	43	1	15.70
85706	10	-	-
85710	40	1	5.20
85711	27	3	6.80
85712	9	2	6.10
85713	24	-	-
85714	5	-	-
85715	21	-	-
85716	28	1	4.80
85717	1	-	-
85718	47	2	6.0
85719	25	2	6.70
85730	17	1	4.50
85732	1	-	-
85736	1	-	-
85737	15	1	5.20
85741	25	-	-
86743	7	-	-
85745	13	-	-
85746	29	1	4.50
85747	6	-	-
85748	4	-	-
85749	23	2	5.20

Air born radon is the second largest cancer killer behind smoking in the United States. During 2001, 5.8 % of the homes built incorporated radon-reducing features-the remainder did not even though radon resistant construction is simple and relatively inexpensive if done during construction(Ref:USEPA). What has Tucson`s elected representatives done to minimize the exposure of citizens to this hazard?

The average new home lot in the Southwest is 6,193 square feet(Ref:review journal .com). The average home size is 2500 square feet . The Potassium 40 beta range exclusion area equals 564 suare feet. The remainder is 3129 square feet or 60 ft x 60 ft. Graywater viral and bacterial impacts on human health are contingent upon design 0f the system.

   In conclusion, graywater insidiously degrades residential property and will insidiously adversely affect the health of household residents-exponentially as duration of time increases.

                                   Respectfully, *Clyde H. Stagner*
                            Clyge H. Stagner, a Tucson citizen

From: "cstampingr@dakotacom.net" <cstamping@dakotacom.net>
To: <mcweb@tucsonaz.gov>
Sent: Wednesday, July 16, 2008 8:48 AM
Subject: Gray water effects on private property

Dear Honorable Mayor and Council Members,
   On 15 July 2008, a copy of a letter,subject as above addressed to the Tucson Pima Water Study, was mailed to each of you.
   My credentials are as follows:
1.1960-62,Chairman,Nuclear and Radiological Defense Committee,US Army Chemical Corp School.
2.1962,Dept. of Defense Radiological Safety Officer,Nevada Test Site
3. 1964,Retirement from US Army as Instructor, Nuclear Weapons Instructor, MOS 8 7330.
4. 1966-68, Pinellas County Health Dept, evaluated radiation from watch repair facilities,color televisions,microwave ovens,and dental facilities(cited by Harvard University).
5 1968-9,Consultant, US Bureau of Radiological Health.
6 1970,BS degree in Engineering,Energy Conversion.
7. 1971-2,Supervisor, Licensing and Regulatory Affairs,Florida Power Corp.,during planning,licensing,and construction of a nuclear power reactor.
8.1990, Nuclear Effects Advisor to the movie,"Blue Sky".
   Only current radiological sampling of the CAP water and the Avra Valley-CAP blend can negate the conclusions contained in the above cited report sent to you. In view of the sixty Tucson Water Dept.monitoring violations cited by USEPA and previously mentioned in a 5 July,2008, communication to you, reliability of results can best be assured by an independant sampling and evaluation labratory for water and sediments in water.
Respectfully. Clyde H. Stagner, a Tucson citizen

From:	"cstampingr@dakotacom.net" <cstamping@dakotacom.net>
To:	<mcweb@tucsonaz.gov>
Sent:	Thursday, July 17, 2008 8:33 AM
Subject:	Health

Dear Honorable Mayor and Council Members,
 Your attention is invited to Mayor and Council Memorandum,Study Session Item #4,dated July 8, 2008, Other Invited Parties.
 Observation of the "Other Invited Parties" indicates no representative of the Pima County Health Dept. has been invited to explain,or define the following:
 Section A0101.14 Irrigation
 "disinfected before irrigation"-explain why edible portion of food plants cannot come into direct contact with gray water-what about graywater mud and little children playing in it? Which is more important:the edible part of food plants or little children?
 Section A0104 Special Conditions:
 (B)"safe and sanitary conditions" define and explain -may negate a judge's interpretation later.
 (C) "greater health threat" in its entirety in lieu of a single analogical example.
 Sincerely, Clyde H Stagner,a Tucson citizen

From:	"cstampingr@dakotacom.net" <cstamping@dakotacom.net>
To:	<mcweb@tucsonaz.gov>
Sent:	Friday, July 18, 2008 10:36 AM
Subject:	Graywater System Failure Rates

Dear Honorable Mayor and Council Members,
 Require Tucson Water Dept.:
 1. to submit ,to the Graywater stakeholders, the annual stastistical failure rate for proposed graywater plumbing within a newly constructed residence and the annual stastistical failure rate for the proposed graywater plumbing installed on the residential lot exterior to the house.
 2. to submit,to the Graywater Stakeholders,the possible,probable,and worst case scenario affects on the human occupants of the residence and the short and long term affects on the constructed residence and the terrestial surface of the residence's lot.
 Publish,on the internet and other media, the final conclusions accepted by the graywater stakeholders.
 Include the final acceptable statistical failure rates,described,supra, as specifications in the Tucson City Code applicable to Gray Water Systems.
 Respectfully,Clyde H Stagner,a Tucson citizen

From:	"cstampingr@dakotacom.net" <cstamping@dakotacom.net>
To:	<info@tucsonpimawaterstudy.com>
Sent:	Saturday, July 19, 2008 10:21 AM
Subject:	rainwater harvesting:businesses & multiplexes

Dear Study Members,
 Require the buildings/complexes cited,supra, to collect rainwater,meter the volume and transport the flowing rainwater to Pima Co Waste Water via sewage system for blending or recharge(paper water credits). In return, the collection entities receive gallon per gallon credits for potable water.Water headed for evaporation has been captured.
 This eliminates local water storage with accompanying health risks, large tanks or cisterns which could adversely affect the aesthetics of Tucson.
 This system would replace City of Tucson's more complex system in proposed city code.
 Respectfully,Clyde h Stagner,a resident of Tucson and Pima County

From:	"cstampingr@dakotacom.net" <cstamping@dakotacom.net>
To:	<mcweb@tucsonaz.gov>
Sent:	Monday, July 21, 2008 11:57 AM
Subject:	Greywater by WHO

Dear Honorable Mayor ang Council Members,

Your attention is invited to,"Overview of graywater management:health considerations,World Health Organization,2006".

For "Bathing and shower", faecal coliform in greywater was 6000 cfu 100 mL;for washing machine(with children) was 26000-845000 cfu 100 mL;for washing machine (without children) was 70-29000 cfu mL; for shower and hand wash was 1500-35000 cfu 100 mL; shower and bath was 10-5000 cfu 100 mL. The number of faecal coliforms cited are well above the accepted safety level. These data demonstrate that greywater could pose a potential health risk to people coming into contact with it(Ref:Page 12) although there are no recorded incidents of serious effects on human health from the reuse of greywater(Page 21).

Accordingly, greywater ,from the sources cited on Page 12, is a Reclaimed Class A+ or Class A requiring warning signage at each bibb and front yard of each residence in accordance with the provisions of Arizona Administrative Codes,Title 18,Ch. 9,Page 96, Sept. 30,2005.

From among the risk minimizations listed,the following are signifigant to the proposed graywater use in Tucson:

-Graywater should not be used in a manner that may result in direct contact with vegetables or other edible plants. It may be used to irrigate fruit plants where the fruit does not make contact with graywater.

-The land application system must be signposted to advise that graywater is being reused and that contact with the water must be avoided.

-Greywater should not be stored,unless it has been treated and disinfected.

Among the effects of greywater on human health are:

-by accidental ingestion of contaminated water during recreational activities.

-by inhalation of aerosoles or dust due to irrigation wiyh greywater.

-by vectoring from infected individuals.

The presence of cations(Ref:Table 7,Page 20) usually enhances the retention of viruses by soil(sic,Tucson Water`s potable water TDS has high cation counts of calcium and magnesium).

Also applicable:

-System flow rates on course sandy soil or gravel should be designed carefully to avoid greywater leaching into ground water or surface water(sic,what is put on the residence lot,stays on the lot).

-Manufacturers of mechanical greywater reuse systems must adequately demonstrate to the satisfaction of the Dept. of Health that the system can be operated effectively in the long term without blockage(sic,what is the annual statistical failure rate? Washing machine lint and TDS on the deposition gravel must be evaluated).

-GREYWATER SHOULD BE USED IN QUANTITIES THAT CAN BE TAKEN UP BY THE PLANTS AND SOIL. EXCESS GREYWATER WILL FLOW TO THE GROUNDWATER AND MAY CAUSE CONTAMINATION(WHICH TUCSON GOVERNMENTAL ENTITY PROVIDES THIS PROOF?)

-Maintain a horizontal separation distance of at least 2 meters,~6 ft., from any point of a pedestrian path,walking, or recreational area(Page 42).

-For the greywater irrigation of ornamental fruit trees and fodder crops, the following tests and frequencies of testing for greywater reuse are
(Table 15,Page 43):

BOD(5) mg/L	<=240	monthly
TDS mg/L	<=140	monthly

Faecal Coliform cfu 100 mL <=1000 2/monthly

Conclusion(Page 44)

@. The most commonly used indicators of faecaal pollution in greywater are coliforms and entercocci. Several studies have reported high numbers of these organisms which indicate substantial faecal contamination of the gray water

The WHO Overview of greywater management lists 55 references including:USEPA,State of Colorado,Azdeq(Title 18,Ch.9),Alabama State Board of Health,State of Florida Dept. of Health,Hawaiin Dept. of Health,Idaho Div of Environmental Quality,Michigag Dept. of Public Health,Nevada Adopted Regulation R 129-98, and Environmental Development Service,Richmond Valley.

CNN recently published a list of the 100 best places to live in the US. Tucson was absent from yhe list but can be found in the best places to live in the West where Tucson is ranked 95 behind Phoenix and among others (Ref:money.cnn.com/best/bplive/).

Respectfully,Clyde H Stagner, aTucson citizen

8565 Pembrook Drive
Tucson,Az 85715

27 July, 2008

To: Mayor Walkup
   City Council Members   Subject:Graywater Needs
   City Manager
   Acting Director, Tucson Water Dept.
   Citizens Water Advisory Committee
   Director, Development Service Dept.

Honorable Mayor, Council Members, and Citizens of Tucson,
  This communication endorses the residential reuse of gray water in an economic, safe, healthy, sustainable methodology for the Tucson citizen residential lot users of gray water.
  Your attention is invited to the City of Tucson`s proposed: "Residential Gray Water Ordinance". The included Appendix O, 2006 International Residential Code for one and two Family Dwellings, establishes minimum regulations for building, plumbing, mechanical, fuel gas, energy, and electrical provisions. This code does not include minimum regulations for HEALTH and ENVIRONMENT provisions. The latter regulations and provisions can be included in the proposed "Residential Gray Water Ordnance" under the authority contained in A.A.C. R18-9-711 par C, under Type I Permit which reads: "Towns, cities, or counties may further limit the use of gray water, described in this Section , by rule or ordinance".
  A primary method of gray water irrigation is through sub-surface distribution and is the method readily approved in Austin, Texas, *when conditions are suitable* (Ref: Gray water: A Sourcebook for Green and Sustainable Building). In certain parts of Austin, difficult conditions such as steep slopes, poor percolation, proximity to lakes, or other problems may require the services of a licensed Professional Engineer. Sub-surface distribution systems for gray water are required to obtain approval from the local Health Dept. , with best applications for low water demanding landscapes(Ref: Gray water, supra).
  Regulation of site wastewater disposal systems is provided by the Austin-Travis County Health Dept(sic, note the workable relationship between county and city). The rules that govern gray water systems are currently based on modifications of septic system guidelines and use components standard to septic systems(Ref: Gray water, supra). The primary modification is the location of the drain field in the root zone of plants. A sub-surface gray water irrigation system is similar in cost to a downsized septic system for a home(a filter and special emitters are also needed for a gray water drip irrigation systems) with a smaller lot area and size. In Austin, Ordnance # 880310-H & I, Chap. 12-4,1992 Code of the City of Austin, governs the construction, inspection, and approval of all septic tanks *and gray water systems.* Periodic inspections by the Health Dept. occur during installation.
  Black water can occasionally be generated by gray water sources but is less of a concern in sub-surface systems(Ref: A Sourcebook for Green and Sustainable Building). Lot sizes well under one half acre(21,780 sq. ft.) will need professional engineering.
  From the proposed ordnance, "Residential Gray Water Ordnance No_, whereas, gray water is a valuable resource as it makes "double use" of water that otherwise goes down the drain (sic,-and recharged at Clearwater). Gray water systems divert some interior water(sic, graywater) for use in outdoor irrigation. Since recharge of gray water is omitted, this "whereas" defines Evapotranspiration(ET) Systems. A typical ET system consists of a septic tank for pretreatment removal of solids followed by distribution into a shallow sand bed covered with vegetation.
  Note :Section A0101.14, Exhibit A, proposed , "Residential Gray Water Ordinance" requires amendment to eliminate all references to food and replace with Par 3., Type I Permit, A.A.R.18-9-711 which states: *No food plants, except citrus & nut trees.* Another required amendment is: Section AO101.15 (b) which states," Human contact with gray water and soil irrigated by gray water shall be minimized", needs the word *"minimized"to be replaced by the word "avoided"* for compliance with Par 1.,Type I Permit, A. A. R. 18-9-711. A touch of coliforms or radioactive potassium 40 may be a touch too much. These two examples emphasize the need for regulatory compliance personnel checks

and balances with operational personnel.

The Evapotranspiration(ET) in Tucson on July 24 ,2008 was 0.27 inches for the day(Ref;ag.Arizona .edu/AZ/dataMET). There are two contributors to ET:transpiration + evaporation. Transpiration is the loss of water from the leaves of flora. Evaporation ,applicable to gray water, is the evaporative loss of water from the terrain surface. Evaporation of gray water is a waste and anti graywater. Therefore, tanspirations must be designed to equal the daily output of residential graywater: a horti cultural expert is required for the determination of those flora capable of existing and growing in alkaline soil and the square footage of the respective flora necessary to provide a daily transpiration equal to 140 gallons of gray water(typical for a family of two). In addition the selected flora growth pattern must be such as to provide shadow coverage of the terrain surface to eliminate evaporation. The resultant square footage of flora determines the square footage of buried irrigation piping and a factor in determining adequacy of lot size for gray water reuse. *At this time, these parameters have not been presented,or made public,and are therefore nonexistent in support of the City of Tucson`s proposed* , "Residential Gray Water Ordinance". The Tucson City Council is advised to ascertain these parameters before promulgating an ordinance involving the economics of residential home construction, the boundary conditions of gray water reuse, and most importantly, whether that residential reuse of graywater is feasible/possible.

Tucson water contains dissolved solids(TDS) reigning in the 400 mg/L concentration. WHO Graywater Management(Page 43) cites a permitted limit of <or=140 mg/L for graywater reuse. Phoenix has levels of TDS over 800 mg/L. Tucson Water Dept. tells the citizens of Tucson that the concentration of TDS will continue to increase as the % of CAP increases. The elected council of Tucson has done nothing to promulgate a maximum allowable concentration of TDS in potable water. The USEPA recommends a maximum TDS of 500 mg/L. Lint and TDS will clog the irrigation pipe orifices. The daily amount of TDS passing through an orifice can be determined from the total orifices vis-à-vis the total daily gray water residential output. Again, the horticultural expert is needed to determine the impact of subsurface salty TDS buildup on the growth sustainability of the previous selected flora. This analysis should include evaluations for 400, 500, 600, 700,and 800 mg/L concentrations, respectively, over a span of ten years. Again, the Tucson City Council is advised to ascertain the results of this analysis before promulgating an ordinance which encourages a Tucson citizen to spend approximately $2,500 for a gray water reuse system. Additionally, the possibility of system failure causing a public health threat,liability.and maintenances issues, and potential negative environmental effects are central concerns in considering approval of innovative systems-the Austin Health Dept. has a cook book of acceptable grey water designs.

In lieu of mechanical failure rate data concerning graywater systems, data on septic tanks is considered. US Census reported 403,000 septic system breakdowns in 1997 and an annual failure rate of 0.065 or 65 breakdowns per 1000 homes annually(Ref: USEPA 675-R-00-08). Response and recovery plans are essentail to control leaks of coli form and interococci-and possible radioactivity if subsurface is involved.

Viruses can be found in gray water, the numbers of fecal coliforms found in gray water were well above the accepted safe level water(WHO Overview of gray water management:health considerations). Every reference concerning residential reuse of gray water, including the State of Arizona, cites the health risks of the system. WHO recommends ,for a sub-surface irrigation system, monitoring TDS levels monthly and coliform twice a month. The Pima County Health Dept. should be consulted for a frequency of bacterial monitoring adjustable to count levels measued by the Pima Dept. of Environmental Quality. Radioactive Potassium40 has been measured in the Colorado River at Toprock, Az, above the entrance to CAP. Annual monitoring for gamma activity three feet above irrigation piping should be randomly conducted at operable gray water systems by the Pima County Dept. of Environmental Quality.

Since the proposed, "Residential Gray Water Ordinance" requires stub-outs/bibbs to be included in residence construction for the installation enhancement of gray water reuse systems, the City of Tucson should provide the following supporting services by the Development Services Dept:

1. Upon pouring of a residential foundation, conduct lot percolation test and terrain surface analysis, and

63

2. Upon finding the lot acceptable for graywater reuse, determine

3. If lot size can accommodate the necessary transpiration flora to absorb all graywater from the residence,and

4. If the lot is accommodating, issue a certified plat delineating(outline) the acceptable lot area for installation of sub-suface irrigation piping accompanied by an annotation stipulating the choices of flora and necessary square footage of horizontal coverage to: a. the construction entity on the residence construction permit and b. the owner of the property

5. With copies forwarded to the Pima County Health Dept. and the Pima County Dept of Environmental Quality.

ADDENDUM

In Aug 1967, three years after retiring as an Instructor, Nuclear Weapons, from the U.S.Army, the undersigned, accompanied by a senior year dental student, radiologically surveyed every dental office in Pinellas County , Fla, to include all towns and cities therein which harmoniously cooperated. An Internet Reference is : The Radiation Control for Health and Safety Act of 1968: History George R McCall & Clyde H Stagner: Report of initial Survey of Dental X-Ray Units, Pinellas County (Fla) Health Dept. reprinted in 1967 House of Representatives (Ref: leda.law.Harvard.edu/leda/data/792/Tran06).

Respectfully, *Clyde H Stagner*

Clyde H Stagner

cc: Tucson City Clerk
   Director, Pima County Health Dept.
   Director, Pima County Dept. of Environmental Quality
   Any citizen, including Stakeholders
   Author

From:	"cstampingr@dakotacom.net" <cstamping@dakotacom.net>
To:	<mcweb@tucsonaz.gov>
Sent:	Tuesday, July 22, 2008 2:12 PM
Subject:	Graywater Public Relations

Dear Honorable Mayor and Council Members,
   In Tucson residential(R-1) development,a lot of 7,000 sq. ft. contains a residence occupying an average of 2,500 sq. ft.. Plotting,on this size lot,a horizontal two dimensional outline of this size home, with frontal and side code setbacks,leaves the remainder of the lot for the exhibition of an actual graywater distribution system. Four leaching lines of which one open line is bottomed by gravel over which runs a graywater pipe line, a second open line in which the graywater pipeline is covered by gravel, a third line covered by the visible surface material,and a fourth line over which are planted several of the recommended flora from":Overview of graywater management health considerations,World Health Organization.2006".
   Such exhibits for a two person family;a three person ,and a four person, residence would provide an orientation facility to show new homeowners what the graywater system would look like on their newly purchased property with the appropriate graywater warning signs.
   An additional convincing public relations effort would be pictures of each Tucson Council Member setting the example by standing with their families beside their graywater residential distribution system on their residential property.
   Displaying these pictures at the exhibition site,supra, and in tourist publications would certainly tout graywater.
   Respectfully.Clyde H Stagner,a Tucson citizen

From:	"cstampingr@dakotacom.net" <cstamping@dakotacom.net>
To:	<TW_WEB@tucsonaz.gov>
Sent:	Wednesday, July 23, 2008 8:54 AM
Subject:	Fw: Residential graywater city code

info-clyde
----- Original Message -----
From:
To:
Sent: Wednesday, July 23, 2008 8:25 AM
Subject: Residential graywater city code

Dear Honorable Mayor and Council Members,
   Yesterday` rainwater harvesting forum revealed a signifigant flaw in the City of Tucson`s mandating process.
   The Federal Government,many years ago, inaugarated the Environmental Impact Statement(personnally worked on nuclear reactor EIS for Florida Power Corp. in 1971) which included all paramaters adversely affecting business,production,and citizens to include cost/benefit analysis. Compared to the Federal protocol,the City of Tucson`s appears to be a rapid procumbent process of effort. This morning`s Arizona Daily Star display`s responsive results of yesterday`s rainwater harvesting meeting
   Certain Tucson City Codes are simple,such as residence setback, but complex in determination with results of little impact on the health,expenses,productivity,sustainability, and environment-these codes can be promulgated with minimum explanation, specification,and enforcement.
   Such is not the situation with Rainwater Harvesting and Graywater Reuse.
   The reuse of rainwater and graywater is intended, by the promulgators, for the greater good. Providing the details and protocol of attainment beforehand to those affected enhances solidarity and trust by placing responsibility and accountability in public view.
   Respectfully,Clyde H Stagner,a Tucson citizen

From:	"cstampingr@dakotacom.net" <cstamping@dakotacom.net>
To:	"Fernando Molina" <Fernando.Molina@tucsonaz.gov>
Sent:	Wednesday, July 23, 2008 1:23 PM
Subject:	Re: Water Harvesting/Greywater -Referal Nos.32300-34407/32252-34350/32299-34406

Dear Mr. Molina,

Sometimes standards change for a better overall result-will send you a report on WHO and graywater in which a graywater analysis exits perhaps different from AZDEQ and Tucson Water-their are different responsibilities other than standards. The proposed graywater ordnance is loaded with plumbing standards before promulgation.

Respectfully,your response is appreciated and Tucson Water`s posture is understood-completely understood. Pima County Health Dept.`s position is lacking-WHO cites multiple Heal\th Departments.

Again,respectfully,a reply to this email is unnecessary-clyde
----- Original Message -----
From: "Fernando Molina" <   >
To: <   >
Cc: "Mary Leon" <   >
Sent: Wednesday, July 23, 2008 12:30 PM
Subject: Water Harvesting/Greywater -Referal
Nos.32300-34407/32252-34350/32299-34406

From:	"cstampingr@dakotacom.net" <cstamping@dakotacom.net>
To:	"Mitch Basefsky" <Mitch.Basefsky@tucsonaz.gov>
Sent:	Wednesday, July 23, 2008 3:49 PM
Subject:	Re: Response to your information regarding graywater

Dear Mr. Basefsky, In this morning`s Az Daily Star,the reporter cited concerns about standards preceeding the promulgation of the proposed Gray Water Recycling Code. Upon reading the proposed code,you shall find a multitude of plumbing standards-why are not the applicable health and environmental standards also included in the proposed code? -clyde
----- Original Message -----
From: "Mitch Basefsky" <Mitch.Basefsky@tucsonaz.gov>
To: <cstamping@dakotacom.net>
Cc: "Martha Vanwinkle" <Martha.Vanwinkle@tucsonaz.gov>; "Mary Leon"
<Mary.Leon@tucsonaz.gov>; <Marcel.CHRO/CHROM?@tucsonaz.gov>;
<Ward1@tucsonaz.gov>; <Ward2@tucsonaz.gov>; <Ward3@tucsonaz.gov>;
<Ward4@tucsonaz.gov>; <Ward5@tucsonaz.gov>; <Ward6@tucsonaz.gov>
Sent: Wednesday, July 23, 2008 2:50 PM
Subject: Response to your information regarding graywater

From:	"cstampingr@dakotacom.net" <cstamping@dakotacom.net>
To:	<mcweb@tucsonaz.gov>
Sent:	Friday, August 01, 2008 9:39 AM
Subject:	Unacceptable advice for disease control

Honorable Mayor and Council Members,

At the 31 July Graywater Stake holders meeting, the city staff was queried as to where a mother would/should wash an infant's fecally soiled cloth diaper(not allowed to be washed in washing machine in graywater system proposed code).

A member of the city staff responded: by turning a valve,the mother could wash the cloth diaper in the washing machine and the soiled water would go into the sewage system, This was the complete answer in the presence of a mother with a chest held baby.

Reasons for unacceptable advice:

1. The polio virus is shed from the intestine of every baby who has received the oral polio vaccine. The discarded human waste contains bacteria and viruses(Ref:The ecological debate: cloth vs. disposable;geocities.com/Wellesley/atrium/8608/cloth-vis-diposable).

2. An infant's feces and urine can contain any of over 100 viruses, including polio and hepatitus from vaccine residues.(Ref:Consumer's World;Do Disposble Diapers Ever Go Away?,Michel D. Hinds, The New York Times,Dec. 1988).

3.The composition of fecal flora in healthy infants consists of approximately 20 genera and 100 species(Ref: MAMANEH,Malasia Association of Material and Neonatal Health).

The unacceptable advice consists of failure to include the requirement to disinfect the washing machine after washing fecal contaminated clothe diapers.

IMPRESSION:Since the above answer was based on plumbing turn of the valve and the City Staff has yet to respond to Safety,Environmental and Health concerns associated with graywater reuse:

The City of Tucson elected representatives and city staff want accolades for a first time residential graywater reuse ordnance without accepting responsibility and accountability for what occurs outside the residence over the passage of time.

The City of Tucson elected representatives cite graywater reuse as on lot volitional which hangs responsibility and accountability on the residential lot owner/occupant.

Later system complaints,adverse health affects, system failures , and disease shutdowns, can be expressed as an albatross around the neck of the stakeholders.

Respecfully with citizen disappointment, Clyde H Stagner,a Tucson citizen

From:	"cstampingr@dakotacom.net" <cstamping@dakotacom.net>
To:	<Rodney.Glassman@tucson.gov>
Cc:	"Tony Davis" <verdin@azstarnet.com>
Sent:	Thursday, September 18, 2008 8:46 AM
Subject:	Guest Opinion

Dear Honorable Councilman Rodney Glassman,

Placing gray-water conservation in the hands of the homeowner could have been accomplished by promulgating a city code requiring the new home builder to offer the optional gray-water plumbing as an option to the new home buyer. Installation of the gray-water plumbing in speculative homes would be the option of the builder.

The city council has yet to realize its resposibility and accountability to promulgate a code standard regulating the Total Dissolved Solids(TDS) in Tucson potable water. The Tucson Water Dept. states the dissolved solids in Tucson's potable water will increase as the % of the contaminated CAP water increases in the potable(?) blend. Increases in TDS are related to deterioration in plumbing and household appliances.

My family and friends visiting Tucson shall be advised:

Don't buy a home in Tucson with unnecessary plumbing unless it's optional and desireable.

Don't drink the water.

Respectfully, Clyde h Stagner,a resident of your ward

From: "cstampingr@dakotacom.net" <cstamping@dakotacom.net>
To: <mcweb@tucsonaz.gov>
Sent: Sunday, August 03, 2008 11:39 AM
Subject: Graywater

Honorable Mayor and Council Members,

By the year 2025, and thereafter except for outstanding water credits, the annual withdrawal of water from an aquifer may not exceed the annual recharge. The annual natural recharge of the Tucson Basin is 66,000 acre-ft per year (Ref:Water Resources in the Tucson Basin,ag.arizona.edu/SWES/tucson).. Based on the 2000-2002 average annual storage increase of 35,000 acre-ft per year(Ref: Groundwater Users Advisory Council minutes, Tucson Active Management Area, Dec 7, 2004), the Avra Valley natural groundwater recharge is 17,500 acre-ft per year. The total possible available groundwater annually, based on 2008 water resources, is equal to:

66,000 acre-ft/yr + 17,500 acre-ft/yr = 83,500 acre-ft/yr

plus the CAP allotment of 135,000 acre-ft/yr(possibly 144,000 acre-ft/yr) gives a total of:

83,500 acre-ft/yr + 135,000 acre-ft/yr = 218,500 acre-ft/yr.

This is Tucson Water`s total annual user available water total in acre-ft/yr (unless other water sources are obtained).Sustainability involves keeping the 218,500 acre/ft per year available for use.

Evaporation is the primary concern affecting the increase or decrease of the total cited,supra. Rainwater harvesting and collected water from air conditioning units can increase the total acre-ft/yr cited ,supra. Graywater reuse will reduce the total available acre-ft/yr.

Graywater is discharged only in areas where there is at least five feet between the point of discharge and the ground water table to protect ground water resources from possible contamination(Ref.Gray Water Irrigation Guide, Mar 19, 2003, nmenv.state.nm.US/OOTS/Gray%Water%20Irrigation%20Guide1). In 1971.on the Eckard College Campus,under the auspices of a Doctorate in Microbiology, funded by Florida Powwer Corporation, and witnessed by the undersigned, viable virus traveled through 14 feet of sloping earth in a period of two weeks(albeit their number was greatly reduced).

The proposed Tucson Graywater reuse Code endorses a possible maximum residential graywater production to Evapotranspiration which is:

Evapotranspiration=transpiration+evaporation

  =flora leaf evaporation+ground evaporation

  =total evaporation

  =total residence graywater

which is a loss from the 218,500 acre-ft/yr

Should all new residential home owners avail themselves of Tucson`s graywater incentives, follow city employee graywater promotional efforts, and install graywater reuse systems, the loss of water is determined as follows:

Population served by Tucson Water in 2008 was 750,000(Ref: extrapolated from Fig. 2.3, 2008 Update to Water Plan:2000-2050,Tucson Water Dept.). Estimated Long Range Planning population to be served in 2030 is 1,405,799 (Ref:Water Plan 2000-2050,Tucson Water. The increase in population between 2008 and 2030 is equal to 655,799. The average size family is three persons(Ref:Census 2000,Demographic Profile highlights) and

(655,799 persons)/(3 individuals/household)= 218,600 households

The amount of daily graywater per household equals 118 gal/household/day (Ref:Water Resources Availability for the Tucson Metropolitan Area,barbaralasky.com/tucson-water) and

(118 gal/household/day)x218,600 households=25,794,800 gal graywater/day and

25,794.800 gal/dayx365day/yr = 9415.102 million gal/yr and

(9415.102 million gal/yr)/(325,851 gal/acre-ft)=

28,890 acre-ft /yr loss of water to atmosphere.

Repeating the computations for Tucson Water Service Area long range planning population of 1,483,649 in 2050 results in a 32,320 acre-ft/yr loss of water which is 14.79 % of total available.

The total available water in 2025 of 218,500 acre-ft/yr is a constant: the graywater annual water loss is a variable related to the increase of residences installing graywater systems.

There are mitigating solutions other than plumbing involving responsibility and accountability. What scientific evidence does the City of Tucson/PimaCounty have for the avoidance of all known best method disinfection technology for wastewater prior to recharge which San Diego and Los Angeles are considering?

Las Vegas and Henderson,Nev are sending disinfected wastewater back into Lake Mead from whence it came. The citizens of Tucson are drinking their waste water. Thanks to Prop.200 and the citizens of Tucson,CAP water is recharged-no thanks to Tucson Water Dept.

Respecfully, Clyde H Stagner, a Tucson citizen

The population, served by the Tucson Water Dept. in 2008, was 750,000(Ref:extrapolation from Fig. 2.3, 2008 update to Water Plan:2000-2050, Tucson Water Dept). The estimated long range planning population to be served in 2030 is 1,405,799 (Ref: Water Plan 2000-2050,Tucson Water Dept). The increase in population between 2008 and 2030 is 655,799. The average size family is three persons (Ref: Census 2000,Demography Profile Highlights) and,

   (655,799 persons)/(3 persons/household) = 218,600 households.

Tucson water use is 274 Gallons per Household per Day(GPHD) for homes built since 2000 (Ref:Global Profession Services,Inc, for John Wesley Miller Companies). Thirty three per cent (33%) of household water is used for bathing (USEPA,1992) and twenty one per cent (21%) for cleaning (Ref: How We Use Water in These United States,USEPA) the sum of which totals 54% going to graywater and,

   247 gal water/household/day x 54% graywater/water = 133.38 gal graywater/household/day

   133.38 gal graywater/household/day x 365 days/yr = 48683.7 gal graywater/household/yr

   48683.7 gal graywater/household/yr x (3.06888 x 10^-6 acre ft/gal = 0.14940443 acre ft graywater/household/yr

   0.14940443 acre ft graywater/household/yr x 218,600 households = 32,570 acre ft graywater/yr to envirotranspiration

Envirotranspiration results in an annual loss of a water quantity, in this case 32,570 acre ft, from the toatal available water inventory: this vlume is not available for effluent, effluent recharge for irrigation, or recharge to obtain potable water.The Tucson Active Management Area (TAMA) cites, from the present through 2025, an annual evapotranspiration budget of 3,700 acre ft budget loss , mainly in the Upper Santa Cruz. Promulgation of a city code with the intent of enticing the use of residential graywater can have the result of slowly inceasing increasing the annual loss of graywater in 2010 to an ultimate 32,570 acre ft/yr (22.6 % of present CAP allocation). Each residential graywater/flora system necessitates specific design-there are no requirements for matching residential graywater quantity to residential irrigation quantity needs with the conclusion that all graywater goes to envirotranspiration.

    Respectfully,Clyde H Stagner,a citizen of Tucson and Pima County

---

cstampingr@dakotacom.net

From:	"cstampingr@dakotacom.net" <cstamping@dakotacom.net>
To:	<mcweb@tucsonaz.gov>
Sent:	Saturday, September 27, 2008 10:43 AM
Subject:	Politics vs Water

Dear Honorable Mayor and Tucson Councilpersons,
   The increase in population between 2008 and 2030 is estimated to be 655,799. With an average size family of three persons, the increase in households is 218,600. The $500.00 per residence for stub-out plumbing represents $109,300,000 in additional monetary input into Tucson for vendors,plumbers,and tax receipts. Should all residences install $5,0000.00 graywater systems, an additional input of $1,093,000,000 would flow into the Tucson economy during the period 2010-2030.
   For this same period, Mr Tannler, Director ADWC,Tucson TAMA, has been apprised that the TAMA water budget's annual riparian (evapotranspiration) water budget loss of 3,700 acre-ft annually could increase by 28,890 acre-ft annually due to residential graywater riparian(evapotranspiration) water loss. The potential residential graywater loss is equal to 20.06 % of Tucson's annual allocation of CAP surface water.
   During the past several months, email correspondence has been received from Mr. Jeff B. Biggs, newly appointed Director of the Tucson Water Dept.. In every message, Mr. Biggs has been forthright, helpful, and responsive with conclusive remark offering help with any additional problem or comment offered. Mr. Biggs gives facts without equivocation. His assistance was, and is, thankfully appreciated.
   My gratitude to the Mayor ,Tucson Councilpersons, and the Tucson governmental protocol for allowing,considering, and responding to a citizen's viewpoints,scientific input, and concerns over the past several months.
   Respectfully, Clyde H Stagner, a Tucson citizen.

From: "cstampingr@dakotacom.net" <cstamping@dakotacom.net>
To: <mcweb@tucsonaz.gov>
Sent: Wednesday, June 25, 2008 4:22 PM
Subject: FAHRENHEIT 104

Dear Honorable Mayor and Council Members,
  In a Tucson residence, the shower head is connected to the hot water heating tank by a 3/4 inch pipe 100 feet in length although the length is a variable for other Tucson homes.Turning on the shower results in the 100 foot length pipe being emptied of water which is replaced with hot water from the tank heater. Forty feet of 3/4 inch pipe holds 1 gallon of water: a hundred foot pipe holds 2.5 gallons of potable water, which in this case ,goes down the drain. This potable water loss can be reduced by shortening the 100 foot length of 3/4 inch pipe between the showerhead and the hot water tank.
  Some hot water tank manufacturers preset the tank thermostat to 140 F. Hot water in tanks is usually heated by gas,propane, or electricity-in some electrical heating tanks the thermostat is factory set and contained in covered compartment difficult to access-140 F may damage electrical components.Most Jacuzzis have water temperatures of 104 F.Most people shower or bath at temperatures between 98 F and 104 F(Ref:Go Tankerless Water Heater Co.). The human skin is sensitive to water temperature and tolerates 104 F-higher temperatures may scald.
  When a Tucson resident turns on the shower water, the hot water must be cooled by mixing with potable 79 F water(Ref:Your Water Connection,Tucson Water,June 2008) which is transported to the shower in a separate 3/4 inch pipe.The number of potable water gallons required for mixing with the heated water to attain a mixture of 104 F is determined by:
  1gal(140F)+ y gal(79F)=(1+y)(104F)=144gal
Turning on the shower to a preset temperature location causes 1.44 gal of 79 F water to flow simultaneously for each gallon of water being initially purged from the hot water pipe line.The total 79 F water is 2.5x1.44=3.6 gal of potable water which is purged and wasted at every shower.
  If all Tucson water tank heaters were set at 140 F,the toatal wasted potable water would be: Population Gal/waste/day Acrefeet/year

Population	Gal/waste/day	Acrefeet/year
500,000	1,800,000	2,020
1,000,000	2,600,000	4,040

  Standby loss accounts for 20 to 60 % of total tank heater cost.For a residential use of 100 heated gallons of water a day heated to 140 F from 79 F,the cost is:
100galx8.33lbs/galx1BTU/lbx(61)=50813BTU
$1.032/thermx50813BTU/100,000BTU/therm=$0.51
Using 40% as standby loss of total,0.51=0.6 T
and T=$0.85 total daily cost for heated water.
  Repeating the calculations for 79 F to 104 F results in a total cost of $0.37 Reducing the hot water temperature maximum temperature from 140 F to 104 F saves $0.14daily=$50.40 annually.
  Consideratons:Only install electrical dishwashers equipped with water temperature booster to 140 F(detergent dependant).A temperature of 104F is tolerable and saves the additional water required cool the hot water.Washing machines can use cold water detergent-washing clothes in cold water has gone on for centuries with satisfactory results.Sustaining Tucson citizens is Tucson sustainability-FAHRENHEIT 104.
  Respectfully,Clyde H Stagner,a Tucson citizen

CHAPTER 8

BOTTLED POTABLE WATER

Tucson Water shall offer to provide wholesale water service to other retail water providers in the region. Tucson Water shall be responsible for delivering wholesale water in accordance with the primary water quality standards established pursuant to the Federal Safe Drinking Water Act (Ref:42 United States Code Section 300 and et seq) at the point of delivery to the retail water service provider (Ref: Tucson Water System Status Report 2007, Page 12, Par 6).

What is the Tucson Water Department cost, including Capital, Debt, Operating, and Product, to produce and deliver one gallon of potable water?

From: "cstampingr@dakotacom.net" <cstamping@dakotacom.net>
To: <mcweb@tucsonaz.gov>
Sent: Monday, June 30, 2008 11:31 AM
Subject: bottled water

Dear Honorable Mayor and Council Members,
  Tucson tourists and business associates arriving at the Tucson Municipal Airport view a conglomerate of citizens-many toting plastic bottles of water. A similar sight is observed on the University of Arizona campus- and in city,county, and federal buildings. What an endorsement for Tucson Water Dept. Does the county and city allow their employees to purchase bottled water with taxpayer funds?Does stacked bottled water in Tucson retail outlets denote sustainability to Tucson visitors?
  Tucson Water estimates 60% to 65% of its municipal customers don`t drink tap water.Why? Tucson Water Dept. wholesales potable water to the following bottlers of water in Tucson(Ref:Internet):
  Miraval
  Water Street Station
  Coca Cola Bottling Co. of Tucson
  Water West(2 locations)
  C&S Water Mart
  Culligan/ Oasis Water
  Sparklet`s Water
  Kalil Bottling Co.
  Usually the water bottler uses reverse osmosis(RO) twice and then sterilizes the water. Twice as much water is used in production of a bottle of water than the bottle contains(Ref:Pacific Institute). In 2005, bottled water consumption was 99 liters per US citizen(Ref: Worldwatch Institute). The US Census estimated Tucson`s 2005 population as 518,956.
  Converting two wasted liters of water(per one bottled) to quarts = 2.1134 quarts = 0.528 gal
 518,956x0.528x99=27,126,867gal=83.26acre-ft
of Tucson potable water wasted annually.
  Tucson Water Dept`s water cost rate for commercial, all usage, is $1.71 per ccf = $1.71per 748 gal = 0.0023 cents a gallon. Is the City of Tucson subsidizing private enterprise at the expense of its tax paying citizens? Does the City of Tucson stock the Tucson Food Bank with bottled water for the homeless and indigents? Foe emergencies?
  Mental degrading of Tucson water quality can cause citizens to install(personal experience) reverse osmosis (RO) units which recover only 5 to 15% of the water entering the system:the remainder is discharged as waste water.An RO unit delivering 5 gal of treated water per day may discharge 40 to 90 gal of waste water per day (Ref:Wikipedia,internet).
  Tucson,with its friendly citizens,and beautiful terrestial cleanup,could do well with award winning clean water. Sustainability of the citizens of Tucson is Tucson sustainability.
 Respectfully,Clyde H Stagner,a Tucson citizen

From:	"cstampingr@dakotacom.net" <cstamping@dakotacom.net>
To:	<mcweb@tucsonaz.gov>
Sent:	Thursday, July 03, 2008 10:26 AM
Subject:	bottled water

Dear Honorable Mayor and Council Persons,
 Chicago is the first major city to tax bottled water according to the Chicago Tribune. Chicago will start charging an extra five cents per bottle of water(Ref:Thedailygreen,Thursday,July 3, 2008).
 San Francisco and Seattle have banned purchases of bottled water by their city governments (Ref:cbs5.com/local/newsom.bottled.water).
 A dozen New York City hotels and restaurants have banned bottled water(Ref:NewYorkPost,July 3, 2008).
 Ann Arbor,Mich, passed a resolution barring city vendors from selling commercial bottled water at city events. The city is selling reusable water bottles that can be filled with tap watere (Ref:autobloggreen.com/2007/07/16/ann-arbor-moves-to-ban-bottled-water-sale-from-city-events/-69k).
 Requiring plastic water bottles to be manufactured with at a minimum of 40% recyclable plastic is also an option for sustainability.
 Tucson presently has a dual system for providing potable water. One part of the system wholesales potable water which goes through reverse osmosis and resold as bottled potable water(with two bottles of potable water wasted for each bottle sold) to the affluent:the second part retails water with higher TDS to the remainder of Tucson citizens.Tucson Water states 70% of their customers have no complaints:why are so many bottles of water being sold and consumed in Tucson.
 Sustainability of Tucson bottled water and its sales has been expressed-is this sustainability of Tucson citizens and Tucson sustainability?

From:	"cstampingr@dakotacom.net" <cstamping@dakotacom.net>
To:	"Mitch Basefsky" <Mitch.Basefsky@tucsonaz.gov>
Sent:	Wednesday, July 09, 2008 2:43 PM
Subject:	Re: Response to your comments regarding bottled water

Dear Mr. Basefsky,
 Only one Wholesale recipient was cited- that recipient is a customer of potable water producer Tucson Water who resells potable water as potable water.
 Please correct the following if incorrect. The water used by Tucson Water is the property of the citizens of Tucson and not the property of the Tucson Water Dept.
 The home owner using a reverse osmosis who wastes potable water does so using his property without making a profit. Tucson Water`s selling of potable water to a potable water wholesaler transfers ownership of potable water from the citizens of Tucson to another entity.
 My wife has had one kidney removed in 1992 (in Tucson) due to cancer. In 2002,she had radical abdominal surgery for colon cancer removal which left her with a stent from bottom of remaining kidney(which is 10% functional) to top of bladder. This stent must be surgicall replaced every nine months.
A reverse osmosis system is operating in our home and,Mr. Basefsky, we are wasting water to save a life-not make a profit from selling nutrient deficient water.
 Please advise where the specific water quality data for Avra Valley can be viewed-2006 and 2007 data if convenient.
 Thanks-clyde
----- Original Message -----

73

>>>> "   " <
> PM >>>
> Dear Mr.Basefsky,
> Thank you for the response.The content was histotically interesting.
> Has
> anyone discussed with counsel the legality of charging more for sales
> of
> potable water to wholesale customers.
> Tucson Water`s sales to residential customer is not done so for
> resale.
> Tucson Water`s sales of potable water to commercial customers for
> resale
> is wholesale.How about an wholesale water waste fee?
> Your response indicates absolutely no effort,active or planned, by
> Tucson
> Water
> to achieve energy sustainability by reduction of plastic bottle use in
>
> Tucson or water sustainability by reduction of water waste in the
> supply of
> bottled potable water.
> Your respose quoted a 70% customer satisfaction survey-when
> ,where,who.how
> and why was the survey taken? Where on the internet can the facts and
> references of this survey be perused?
> At a university in this country on this date,an effort to reduce
> potablebottled water use is being evaluated. An installation of
> charcoal
> filters on every public faucet with informative signs thereon and
> repeated
> PR area wide is a volitional choice methodology for sustainability-if
> the
> motivation exists-

> Clyde H Stagner,a Tucson citizen
>

74.

CHAPTER 9

ATMOSPHERIC WATER GENERATORS

Swamp coolers and air conditioners are used extensively for cooling residences in Tucson-especially in the late spring and summer months whe temperatures exceeding 100 F are frequent. Swamp coolers are effective when the relative humidity is low-potable water is used which is distributed after vaporization by heat removal from the incoming outside air.

Air conditioners, using refrigerant, condense water from the incoming hot air water vapor (which requires heat to condense) and distributes cool air through the distribution system. The condensed water vapor is water which either evaporates on the roof or drains to somewhere and evaporates. This water can be collected and added to the water provider`s total water inventory

Residential air conditioners on roofs have electrical connections and gas connections for winter heating. A pipe for condensed water drainage from the roof to the residence sewer line could collect the water. The amount of condensed water is substantial when the temperature and relative humidity conditions are ideal. The amount of water produced by a given air conditioner can be calculated. Another Tucson City Council Plumbing Code is indicated.

Atmospheric Water Generators (AWG) are essentially refrigerant air conditioners designed to produce potable water. AWG units also produce potable water and refrigeration simultaneously rendering their use more cost effective. AWG potable water sources are sustainable water sources albeit quantity variant with temperature and relative humidity.

From: "cstampingr@dakotacom.net" <cstamping@dakotacom.net>
To: <info@tucsonpimawaterstudy.com>
Cc: <mcweb@tucson.gov>
Sent: Sunday, July 20, 2008 12:14 PM
Subject: water recapature

Dear Tucsopimawaterstudy Members,

An average residence is 2500 sq. ft. in surface area and 10 ft. in height(Ref:Wiki Answers) for a volume = 20000 sq. ft.= 566400 Liters.

The density of air at ordinary atmospheric pressure and 25 C = 1.19 g/liter and

1.19 g/L x 566400 L = 674016 g/air

One joule(J) is the amount of energy required to cool one gram of dry air by one degree celsius(C).

On 19 July 2008,the Tucson mean temperature(Ref:AzDailyStar) was 86 F=30 C. For a residence temperature setting of 72 F=22.22 C

throught the 24 hr period,the temperature difference = 7.78 C. The energy required to cool the residence for the consecutive 24 hours is:

7.78C x 1J/Cg air x 674g/air=5243844.4J

Cooling of the residence is accomplished by the transfer of heat to the condensation of water in the air. The amount of energy required equals

2,270,000 joule/kg and

(5243844.4 J) / (2270000 J/kg=2.31 kg of water=2.31 L of water and

2.31 L x 0.2641 g/L=0.61 gal of water/residence

The 2003 US Census for Tucson MSA cites 350,000 occupied houses. In 1992, 19% of residences had only refrigerant cooling and 21% had both. For the date cited,supra, 40 % of residences are assumed to be using refrigerant cooling which is:

350000 x 40% =140000 and

0.61 gal/house x 140000 houses=85400 gal/day=31171000 gal/year=95.66 acre- ft/yr

A more accurate report can be rendered by using up to date census data and the inclusion of business and manufacturing facilities using refrigerant for cooling.

CONCLUSION:The City of Tucson and Pima County should promulgate a code/ordnance requiring all new construction connected to the Pima County sewer system and containing refrigerant cooling to collect and transport the refrigerant water product into the city /county sewage system.

Respectfully,Clyde H Stagner,a citizen of Tucson and Pima County

From:	"cstampingr@dakotacom.net" <cstamping@dakotacom.net>
To:	<info@tucsonpimawaterstudy.com>
Cc:	<mcweb@tucsonaz.gov>
Sent:	Tuesday, September 02, 2008 9:47 AM
Subject:	Water sustaiability:air water generators

Air Water Generators remove vaporized water from high humidity ambient air.Examples are:

Manufacturer	ID	Capacity L/gal	Ideal Conditions, F/%RH	Average Power	Refrigerant	Anti Contaminant	noise,db
Airwatercorp	AW120	120/31.7	68-104 / 60-100	0.1-0.4 kw/hr/L	R407c	UV	*noised-* 65
"	AW 250	250/66	" "	" " "	"	"	"
"	AW500	500/132	" "	" " "	"	"	68
"	Aw1000	1000/264	68-104 / 35-100	0.4 kwhr/L	"	"	69
"	AW5000	5000/1320	68-104 / 60-100	0.1-0.4 kwhr/L	"	"	77
Sustainable Village	NI 11067*	2-13gal		Hot &cold water 771 watts	R134-a	Filter,UV	
AWG	AWG**	120/ 31.7	60/>40	2.6kw		Ozone,filter	

*Cost:$1,399.00
**Cost:$1,400.00

Tucson`s historical temperatures and relative humidity are amenable(Ref:Tucson Weather History-City Rating.com) to the AW 1000 and 264 gallons of water output per day. Excluding June,four months of ~ continuous operation yields 1056 gal and 7 months of ~ 50% operation yields ~ 924 gal for an annual total equal to 1980 gal. For an acre-ft= 325,851.429 gal,the annual water output of 165 of the AW1000 units is required. Based on the pro rata cost from the AWG of $1400 per 31.7 gal, the estimated cost of the Aw1000 for 264 gal output is $11700 and for 165 units is $1,923,785.30. The energy cost for the 165 unit conversion of water vapor to an acre-ft of liquid water is 325,851.429 gal x 1.52 kwhr/gal x 8.4 cents/kwhr = $41,604.71.

With the built in ultraviolet contaminant abater and water practically devoid of Total Dissolved Solids(TDS) and other CAP -groundwater contaminants(some of which could increase in groundwater concentration with successive recharge recyclings),the units should be evaluated for locations adjacent to outlying pumping stations and for subsequent reductions in infrastructure maintenance and replacement costs. The waste water from these units would contribute to the contaminant dilution of the total waste water and continue to do so over time. Installation and operation of sufficient Air Water Generators is possible to meet the potable water drinking demand of present and future Tucson residence requirements-Tucson commercial,industrial, and commercial annual water requirements could be the antithesis of residence welfare. Sustainable adequacy of potable resident drinking water by this methodology could possibly abort future costs of tertiary wastewater treatment(before recharge) by Pima Wastewater Management. A sponsored program,perhaps subdized, endorsing and encouraging the installation of small residential Air Water Generators would further reduce the potble water demand. Installation of Air Water Generators in public and government facilities would further reduce the demand.

The installation, utilization, and quantity evaluations should be accomplished by the Tucson Water Dept. which has expertise in water quantity production.The water quality evaluations should be accomplished by the the Pima County Dept.of Environmental Quality. Cost accounting for future expenditures,maintenance sustainability and future savings based on present worth should be accomplished by a joint team of certified public accountants representing the interests of Tucson,Pima County,and more importantly,both Tucson and Pima County jointly. Air Water Generators are being tested by the military ,are in use in Africa,and in a city government building in Pa- the market is increasing- thorough evaluation of the financial stability of any Air Water Generator manufacturer is necessary before commitment of funds to contract.

A year`s trial run using several Air Water Generators for evaluation by the Tucson Water Dept. is recommended.

Use of Tucson`s abundant solar energy to power Air Water Generators would be sustainably ideal-perhaps sometime in future.

Respectfully,Clyde H. Stagner,a tucson,Pima County citizen

Dear Honorable Tucson Pima Water Study Members,   20 Sept. 2008
PO Box 2344
Tucson, Az 85701   Subject: Cost/Benefit Air Water Generators

Dear Honorable Study Members,
  An email communication entitled, "Water Sustainability: air water generators",
was submitted to the Study Members on 2 Sept. 2008. A reply has been received
from the Water Administrator, Tucson Water Dept. in response to Inquiry-
Assignment No. 34852. The Tucson Water Dept. response is *autoanalysis:* a
comprehensive analysis of the cost/benefits necessitates additional input by
scientific/technological disciplines in addition to those associated with water
production.
  A single Hercules Atmospheric Water Generator capable of producing 3,470
gallons daily of potable water can be ordered from the manufacturer(Infrastructure
Installation Time):
    Model: XZIEX-150-XXA
    Water Output*,**: 3,470 gal/day=1,266,550 gal/yr=3.8868 acre-ft/yr
    Power Input: 195 kwh
    Power Cost***: $15.69/h=$374.40/day=#136,656/yr
    Power Source: 110V/60 Hz; 220V/50 HZ
    Contaminant Control: Sediment Filter
                        Carbon Filter
                        Ultra Violet
                        Ozone injection
   Certification: ISO 9001
                  Qualifies for LEED credits in US only
                  UL Approved
                  Filtration Systems exceed NSF Standards
                  Results of Water Tests available
    Air Conditioner Output*: 36,000 Standard cf/m(SCFM)
                        400cftm=1 ton air cooling capacity
                        36,000cftm=90 ton air cooling capacity
        As a rule of thumb, 400 sqf can be cooled by 1 ton air cooling capacity
                        90 Ton x 400 sqft/ton=36,000 sqft
            Ref: Wikipedia, the free encyclopedia
    A/C Power Savings*** = Power Cost***

    **Based on ideal conditions of 85 F and 70% RH
    ***Computed at 8 cents/kwh for continuous annual operation

  The quantity of potable water output is contingent upon the temperature and
relative humidity. For Tucson climate, a software program for these variables, and
specifications for a particular unit, could compute the total unit potable water
output for a given year. An alternative methodology is the installation of a potable

water generating unit(of lesser capacity) with monitoring of water output vis-à-vis temperature and relative humidity conditions.

Data from another manufacturer of a lesser potable water output of 15.3 gal/day, at maximum at 95 F and 100% RH, cites 1.7 gal/day at 59 F and 50% RH.

Automatic on/off settings for temperature and relative humidity variables reduces operating costs.

Additional potable water output at a given location can be obtained by combining multiples of the XZIEX-150-XXA. For example, 288 units would output ~ 1 million gal/day(~1120acre-ft/yr) and cool ~10,000,000 sqft a day. The Atmospheric Water Generating market is emerging-cost per unit is rarely quoted-costs are negotiable.

Radon deaths from lung cancer in the United States are 21,000 annually(Ref: American Lung Association,Radon Fact Sheet, Sept. 2007). The estimated population of the United States in 2008 is 306.4 million (Ref: Wikipedia, the free encyclopedia). For a one million(MSA) population,Tucson's share of radon deaths is 69 annually.

In 1999, the Tucson Water Dept. had six of thirty reservoirs with radon levels exceeding 300 pCi/L- the National Academy of Sciences and US EPA's recommended maximum concentration in potable water. In 1999, 53 of 153 Points of Entry, Tucson Water Dept., exceeded 300 pCi/L(Ref:Tucson Water Dept., 1999 Point of Entry Radon Levels). The location and radon concentrations of the following Point of Entry/wells are significant:

POE No.	Address	Radon Concentration, pCi/L
AV-001A	7295 S. Sandario Rd	1,230
AV-002A	11001 W. Ajo Way(South)	790
AV-003A	11007 W. Ajo Way(S.Well)	860
AV-005A	6505 S. Sandario Rd.	1,070
AV-006A	11002 W. Ajo Way(North)	1,400
AV-007A	12600 W. Ajo Way(North)	1,078
AV-008A	10200 W. Ajo Way(C Well)	903
AV-009A	10190 W. Ajo Way(S Well)	1,056
AV-011A	10971 W. Park Rd(N Well)	1,210
AV027A	9830 W. Ajo Highway	1,370

What are the present radon levels in the Clearwater CAP blend?

Output from an Atmospheric Water Generator would eliminate the radon killer. In a cost/benefit analysis, what value does the City of Tucson, Tucson Water Dept. place on the lives of 69 Tucson citizens? It is suggested that the citizens of Tucson be asked this question rather than the Tucson Water Dept.

The potable water output of Atmospheric Water Generators contain no Total Dissolved Solids(TDS) which is a Clearwater CAP blend problem for Tucson and Pima County(Ref: Conclusions, The Tucson Basin Desalinization Project, Group 3, 29 Sept. 2005, ag.Arizona.edu/swes/tucwater1/For%20website%20Fall05/Final%20Draft%20Group%203%). A cost/benefit analysis of Atmospheric Water Generators should include the cost savings for the possible elimination, partially or completely, of the CAP blend TDS disposal problem. Should TDS disposal be the responsibility of Pima County, their input into a cost/benefit analysis is crucial and essential in deference to the Tucson Water Dept.

The elimination of other contaminants, such as per chlorate, uranium, K40, endocrine disruptors, pharmaceuticals, sediments, et al(Ref. Clean Colorado River Alliance) should also be included in a cost/benefit analysis.

Other considerations for inclusion are the benefits of Atmospheric Water Generators under/in the following circumstances/events:

1. Drought impacts on supply of Colorado River water.

2. Uranium contaminations from active mining in Utah and flooding of existing tailings adjacent to the Colorado River.

3. Radioactive contamination of CAP canal water from a nuclear accident at the Palo Verde Nuclear Generating Station.

4. Radiological/chemical/biological contamination of Cap Canal water by domestic or foreign terrorists.

5. Buildup of contaminants in Pima County/Tucson from repeated deposits from recycled water used for potable or irrigative purposes.

6. Cessation of CAP water deliveries due to CAP infrastructure repair/replacement/maintenance.

7. Increase of contaminant to unacceptable concentrations due to increased urbanization and population increases of existing urban areas

Infrastructure savings from flexibility usage of Atmospheric Ware Generators and the cost savings for obtaining air conditioning and potable water for the same kwh cost should be included.

A cost/benefit analysis should be applicable to, and participated in, by all Tucson/Pima County entities subject to expenditures/savings and health/welfare benefits/losses from the use of Atmospheric Water Generators.

Volitional participation by industrial /commercial entities, with incentives, could be an additional source of potable water as a byproduct of air conditioning.

From a citizen of Tucson, please accept my gratitude for the allowance of open expression and participation by expression at your open meetings and by letter/email.

Respectfully, Capt. Clyde H. Stagner, Chemical Corps, U.S. Army, Ret.

From:	"cstampingr@dakotacom.net" <cstamping@dakotacom.net>
To:	<info@tucsonpimawaterstudy.com>
Cc:	<jmlemon01@verizon.net>
Sent:	Sunday, September 21, 2008 7:00 AM
Attach:	xziex%20commercial%20price%20list.pdf
Subject:	Fw: A.W.G. Price List/RH and Temp stats

Dear Honorable Tucson Pima Water Study Members,   21 Sept. 2008
   Your attention is invited to the attachment. Please attach it to the Letter,Cost/Benefit Air Water Generators,dated 20 Sept., 2008 presently enroute to you via US Postal Service.
   Respectfully,Clyde H. Stagner,a citizen of Tucson and Pima County
----- Original Message -----
From: <jmlemon01@verizon.net>
To: <cstamping@dakotacom.net>
Sent: Saturday, September 20, 2008 12:46 PM
Subject: A.W.G. Price List/RH and Temp stats

> Hello Clyde,
>
> Please find attached the price list for all of our units.   The specs
> you requested on unit functionality regarding RH and Temperature are
> included in the list.
>
> I would respectfully request, that all of my contact information be
> forwarded along with this to the Agency that your are submitting it to.
> Unfortunately, there has been numerous problems with others infringing
> on the patents, copyright, etc. I want it to be a matter of record as
> to whom forwarded this information to you, the agency, etc.
>
> John M. Lemon
> Email: jmlemon01@verizon.net
> Phone: 240.210.1022
> Company ID: 1619
> My ID: 11053
> Company ID name: greatwaternow
>
>
> Thank you much. If I can be of any further assistance please let me
> know.
>
> Marc Lemon
>

CHAPTER 10

RECLAIMED WASTEWATER EFFLUENT

The primary sources of Tucson`s reclaimed water effluent are four facilities which produce 15,750 acre-ft/yr. Reclaimed water delivered to Tucson`s customers is a blend of water produced at the city`s Reclaimed Treatment plant, the Sweetwater Recharge Facilities (SFR), the Santa Cruz Managed Underground Storage Facility (SCRMUSF) and Pima County`s Randolph Park Water Reclamation Facility (WRF) with back-up supply from in channel lower Santa Cruz River Managed Recharge Project and Tucson Water`s *potable distribution system* (Ref: Reclaimed Water System Status Report, TWD-2007).The two sources of back-up supply are both based on the ability to add water from the *potable distribution system into reclaimed water reserves at strategic locations- a most comprehensive emergency plan for 14 Tucson golf courses with more soon to come.*

The City of Tucson`s Reclaimed Water System is operated pursuant to policies of the Mayor and City Council. Reclaimed water is under the jurisdiction of the Arizona Department of Environmental Quality (ADEQ) for required tertiary treatment specifications. USEPA has no jurisdiction. Pima County`s Regional Organization Master Plan (ROMP) will define effluent quality (Ref: TWD Reclaimed Water System Report, 6, 2007. Tucson Reclaimed Water Quality, 2007, Class A water (ADEQ) annual averages for inorganic constituents, nitrogen forms, reuse permit and others included a Total Dissolved Solids (TDS) concentration of 658 mg/L

Data information from the Southern Nevada Water Authority shows ozone treatment, 2.5 mg/L, results in <30% removal of Musk Ketone and TCEP and 30-70% removal of meprobamate, atrazine and lopromide. Ultraviolet treatment, UV 40 mJ/cm^2, resulted in less than 30% removal of testosterone, estriol, ethynylestradiol, estrone, astradiol, whereas ozone (2.5 mg/L)removed 100% of these endocrine disruptors but did not completely remove meprobamate, diazepam, or dilantin (Ref: Occurrence, Treatment, and Toxicological Relevance of EDC/PPCPs, clw.CSIRO.air/vido_html/2007/Shane Snyder).

Monitoring of Lake Mead and Las Vegas Wash resulted in maximum concentrations (ug/L)of (Ref: USGS REPORT 02-385, Boyd & Furlong, 2000-2001):

Acetaminophen	0.026
Carbamazepine	0.138
Caffeine	0.140
Cimetidine	0.063
Dehydronefedipine	0.130
Cotinine	0.010
Diltiazen	0.042
Erythromycin	0.184
Sufanethoxazol	0.200
Trimethoprin	0.098

The Southern Nevada Water Authority (SNWA) published annual Water

Quality Summary,2008, for its Alfred Merritt Smith Water Treatment Plant (AMSWTP) and River Mountains Smith Water Treatment Plant (RMWTP). Water quality monitoring data from these treatment facilities indicates which contaminants survive tertiary treatment and subsequently enter Lake Mead , the Lower Colorado River, CAP canal, Tucson, and the citizens of Tucson. Tucson and Pima County, in turn, add additional concentrations to those surviving tertiary treatment and ground water recharge. At the end of the CAP canal (Tucson) these contaminants are recycled over and over with total quantities increasing from continual CAP water inflow. Identification by monitoring is a necessary action for sustainability of CAP surface water use in Tucson.

In fiscal year 2006, 14 golf courses were directly served with effluent by Tucson Water. This effluent constituted 58% of the Reclaimed Water System Total Demand. Another 8% entitlement was distributed to golf courses in Oro Valley. Golf Courses received 10,395 acre-ft (66%) of the total distributed reclaimed effluent (15,750 acre-ft). Schools, parks, and ~700 residences received the remaining 34%. The Near-Term System Growth: FY 2007 through FY 2012 (Ref: TWD Reclaimed Water System Report-2007) cites an increase in reclaimed effluent of 3,748 acre-ft of which 2,867 (75.8%) is for golf courses.

Daylight in Tucson (Ref: US Weather Bureau) is:

MONTH	HRS of DAYLIGHT	LESS PM TIME*	PLAYERS/DAY**
Jan	10.5	6.5	108
Feb	10.36	6.36	104
Mar	11.31	7.31	120
Apr	12.31	8.31	136
May	13.27	9.27	152
Jun	14.07	10.07	160
Jul	14.13	10.13	164
Aug	13.44	9.44	156
Sep	12.49	8.49	140
Oct	11.51	7.51	128
Nov	10.53	6.53	112
Dec	10.20	6.20	100
Maximum number of players annually per golf course>			1,580

*Four hours time to play course limits last T-time befofe twilight.
** Calculations based on four players T-time every 15 minutes of daylight.

For 14 golf courses at maximum number of players a day, a total of 22,120 players were on the 14 golf courses per day. These golf courses used a total of 10,395 acre-ft/yr = 28.48 acre-ft/day = 9,280,248.7 gallons/day. This consumption of effluent equals 419.5 gallons per day per golfer. Excluding Meter Size Rate, the Reclaimed Water usage charge is $1.60 per ccf = 0.214 cents/gal resulting in a cost of 89.77 cents per round of golf.

The cost of reclaimed water produced by the City of Tucson`s Sweetwater facility is $650.00 to $750.00 acre foot of which $100.00 to $150.00 is the cost of production and remainder is for capital costs (Ref: Range of Potential Recharge Needs, VI A 1,TucsonAMA Documents). Using the average reclaimed production cost of $700.00 acre-ft, the cost per gallon equals 0.215 cents per gallon to produce: slightly higher than the price to golf courses.

The reclaimed water rates in 1984 covered 70% of the service costs with the remaining costs paid by potable water costomers (Ref: Reclaimed Water-is it for Everyone, Tom Clark & Karen Dotson,Tucson Water Dept). As an incentive to golf courses, each acre-ft of effluent used is counted at 0.7 acre-ft (Ref;Par for the Course,Christain A. Sierra, Tucson Weekly, Jan 3, 2002). The 70% price reduction results in a golf course cost of 0.1498 cents per gallon: less the potable water cost paid by residential costumers. Affluent Tucson residents play golf: the Tucson Water Dept. and the City of Tucson are subsidizing the affluent at the expense of Tucson citizens,

A Pima County cost of 0.02 cents /gal for reclaimed effluent was derived from Effluent Generation Report, Reclaim Effluent Utilization, Pima County,2007.

In the United states, the number of people who play golf 25 times, or more, a year fell from 6.9 million in 2000 to 4.6 million in 2005 (Ref: Wikipedia, the Free Encyclopedia). In 2006,"pima County asks halt to golf course" (Ref: Az Daily Star, Tony Davis,7/2/2006). "Here are the new courses, now where are the golfers," (Ref: National Golf Tour Letter) Three million golfers quit the game every year (Ref: Pace of Play, internet).

The substitute of effluent and reclaimed water for potable water is an important element in achieving safe yield in the Tucson basin (Appendix A III 2 a (3),Tucson Water Dept. Reclaimed Water System Status Report 2007). This conclusion is auto analytical. It is applicable to achieving safe yield (sustainability) for *potable water*: the Tucson AMA includes many other variables in its water budget for the Tucson Basin and the City of Tucson.

To: Ursula Kramer
Subject: Testing

Dear Ms Kramer,
  Who tests the PCRWRD effluent and sewage sludge for compliance and where can the results be seen.
  Sincerely,
  Clyde H Stagner, Tucson resident

cstampingr@dakotacom.net

From: "cstampingr@dakotacom.net" <cstamping@dakotacom.net>
To: "Ursula Kramer" <Ursula.Kramer@pima.gov>
Sent: Thursday, April 10, 2008 8:34 AM
Subject: Re: Testing

Dear Ursula-thank you and there is question. Recently, the County Manager mentioned sewage effluent,converted to potable water, for future use in Pima County.In such a case, who would test the potable effluent for compliance; Tucson Water or Pima County Waste Management. The answer to this question is related to who is involved for establishing the quality of potable effluent as a first priority before the quantitative use of potable effluent is considered. The infrastructure cost of converting effluent to potable effluent could be several hundred million dollars as Pima County Wastewater Management is now awarein their evaluation of chlorine vis-a-vis ultraviolet. Appreciatively-clyde

From: cstampingr@dakotacom.net [mailto:cstamping@dakotacom.net]
Sent: Monday, April 07, 2008 12:12 PM
To: Jeff Prevatt
Subject: Re: Testing

Dear Mr Prevatt,
  As manager of CROA, please advise of the methodology for a Tucson resident to see the official results of the effluent and sludge pathogenic reports for the years 2005,2006,and 2007.
  What were the final results of the ultraviolet vis-a-vis chlorine disinfection methodologies?
  Sincerely,
  Clyde H Stagner,
  8565 Pembrook Drive
  Tucson,Az 85715

cstampingr@dakotacom.net

From: "cstampingr@dakotacom.net" <cstamping@dakotacom.net>
To: <info@tucsonpimawaterstudy.com>
Sent: Saturday, July 19, 2008 7:46 AM
Subject: Regioanal optimization Master Plan Final Report

Dear TucsonPimaWaterStudy Members,
  Your attention is respectfully invited to the Final Report,cited supra, on which the signature of approval by the Director,Pima Waste Water Management, has yet to be observed.
  The signature of approval denotes authority,resposibility,and accountability for proposal contents in the Final Report in the present and in the future.Preparation of the Final Report by a second party contractor approved ,or recommended, by the Director,Pima Waste Water Management does not include responsibility,accountability,and authority unless so stated in the contractural agreement.
  An additional level of reliability for the citizens of Tucson can be attained by requiring the Superior of the Director,Pima Waste Water Management, to countersign this Final Report.
  Respectfully,Clyde H Stagner,a Tucson citizen

From:	"cstampingr@dakotacom.net" <cstamping@dakotacom.net>
To:	<info@tucsonpimawaterstudy.com>
Cc:	<mcweb@tucsonaz.gov>
Sent:	Friday, September 12, 2008 10:35 AM
Subject:	Pharmaceuticals in Drinking Water:ENVIRONMENTAL NEEDS

Dear Tucson Pima Water Study Members,   12 Sept 2008
  Your attention is respectfully invited to the Arizona Daily Star,"At least 46 million exposed to meds in drinking water",Local Angle, Sept. 12,2008. The Tucson Water Dept`s response did not include the following:

  US EPA states in its guidance(Ref:Federal Register, October 23, 2003,Volume 68, Number 205) that "watershed-based plans should address not only the sources of water quality impairment, but also any pollutants and sources of pollutants that need to be addressed to assure the long-term health of the watershed(sic,citizens of Tucson and Pima County), including both surface and groundwater that serve as sources of drinking water".The Pima Association of Governments(PAG) cites this reference in the endorsements and involvements by the Arizona Department of Environmental Quality(Ref:Watershed Approach to Water Quality Management Planning, pagnet.org/document/water/PC208/ch8_Apr06).THIS PARAGRAPH REQUIRES WATERSHED POLLUTANTS TO BE MONITORED IN ABSENCE OF A US EPA ESTABLISHED MCL STANDARD.

  In 2005, the Govenor of Arizona appointed the Clean Colorado River Alliance to address Colorado River Water Quality. This Alliance selected the following pollutants of concern:
   1. Nutrients(nitrogen,nitrates,ammonia,phosphorus)
   2. Metals(chromium,uranium,copper,mercury,arsenic)
   3. Endocrine disrupting compounds
   4.Perchlorate
   5. Bacteria/pathogens
   6. Salinity/total dissolved solids
   7. Sediment/turbidity

What has Tucson Water Dept. done about these pollutants? Is,THERE IS NO MCL , an answer? Is, AZDEQ`S RESPONSIBILITY,an answer when Tucson Water Dept. is responsible for the potable water for Tucson citizens. Advance weather monitoring is a necessity for hurricane prediction: medical tests provide preliminary warnings of disease,et al.

  Perchlorate well monitoring data for Avra Valley CAP water rechrarge(Ref: AZDEQ:Perchlorates in Arizona,2004)

WELL	PERCHLORATE,ppb
21 CAVSARP	2.4
22 CAVSARP	2.3
9 Avra Valley Recharge	2.4
2-P Avra valley Recharge	2.4

is factual data of Lake Mead`s(containing Las Vegas effluent) contaminant presence in Tucson Water Dept.`s groundwater-CAP blend potable water and contradictory to Chris Avery`s response,at the June 11,2008 Tucson Pima Water Study member meeting in the Copper Room, Randolph Golf Course Club House, that contaminants in surface water are eliminated in the recharge process. Monitoring measurements of Total Dissolved Solids are also contradictory.

  There are three contaminants, Meprobamate(miltown),Diazepram(vallium), and Dilantin which could not be completely removed by treatment with UV 40 mJ, Chlorine 3.5 mg/L, and Ozone 2.5 mg/L at Las Vegas Wastewater Treatment facilities(Ref:Occurrence,Treatment, and Toxicological Relevance of EDC/PPCPs/clw.csiro.air/video_hmtl/2007/ Shane Snyder). The contents of this paragraph should not be considered as all inclusive as pertains to contaminants. Why doesn`t Tucson Water Dept monitor the Avra Valley Groundwater-Cap potable drinking water for these three contaminants? Does CAWCD`s Avra Valley CAP monitoring requirements(permitee) to Arizona Department of Water Resources(permitor) replace any monitoring deemed necessary by the Tucson Water Dept.?

  The City Of Tucson needs an independant Water Quality Dept.

  Respectfully,Clyde H. Stagner,a citizen of Tucson and Pima County

From:	"cstampingr@dakotacom.net" <cstamping@dakotacom.net>
To:	<info@tucsonpimawaterstudy.com>
Sent:	Saturday, July 19, 2008 7:46 AM
Subject:	Regioanal optimization Master Plan Final Report

Dear TucsonPimaWaterStudy Members,
 Your attention is respectfully invited to the Final Report,cited supra, on which the signature of approval by the Director,Pima Waste Water Management, has yet to be observed.
 The signature of approval denotes authority,resposibility,and accountability for proposal contents in the Final Report in the present and in the future.Preparation of the Final Report by a second party contractor approved ,or recommended, by the Director,Pima Waste Water Management does not include responsibility,accountability,and authority unless so stated in the contractural agreement.
 An additional level of reliability for the citizens of Tucson can be attained by requiring the Superior of the Director,Pima Waste Water Management, to countersign this Final Report.
 Respectfully,Clyde H Stagner,a Tucson citizen

CHAPTER 11

WATER SUSTAINABILITY

Tucson has multiples of city employees, citizen organizations, and university proponents touting sustainability. For city employees, sustainability means protecting the pay check. For citizen sustainability organizations control of input and meeting protocol is paramount for city goodwill and contributions. University representatives come in a mixture.

Depending on one`s function, or relationship, sustainability can have a mutitude of definitions and frequently expressed as a fad word with "growth". Sustainability for water depends on the definition of the water involved. The City of Tucson is honed to a quantity sustainability of potable water a quantity of which is forever lost to evaporation and evapotranspiration which is non sustainability for the total annual input of water inventory of Tucson. The Tucson Active Management Area (TAMA) uses the term, "safe yield" for a *gestalt* of nine entities, one of which is the City of Tucson: each with macroscopic water parameters. Tama altered the evapotranspiration loss parameter to riparian loss: is river bank evapotranspiration different from that on a golf course?

The Executive Director, Katherine L. Jacobs, Arizona Water Institute, Univ. of Az., appeared before the Infrastructure, Supply, and Planning Study Oversight Committee known as the Tucson Pima Water Study, and presented several modus operandi for water sustainability. Adaptive Management was explained as requiring knowledgeable expertise in multiple scientific technologies, disciplines, and input data for adjustments to priorities, allocations ,and parameter changes. TAMA`s safe yield water budget parameters whereas Tucson`s are microscopic in comparison. A software program and centralized data storage system are indicated. Continual parameter updating is necessary for environmental, fiscal, quality, quantity, and political water changes made by man or nature.

Tucson water sustainability is a subset of the TAMA safe yield budget which lists and quantifies the macroscopic parameters . Tucson water sustainability, in contradistinction to Tucson potable water sustainability, includes total water quantity input, water evaporation and evapotranspiration, and water transport out of the system which provides a residual quantity available for prioritizing and allocating.

In 2025, Tucson`s annual water input consists of the Tucson Basin`s natural recharge of ~66,000 acre-ft, Avra Valley`s natural recharge of 17,500 acre-ft ,and Tucson`s CAP allocation of 144,000 acre-ft for a total of 227,000 acre-ft.

Tucson`s annual water losses , based on 2008 quantities, except gray water include: Pima County effluent discharge of 60,260 acre-ft., Pima Parks and Recreation irrigation of 4,377 acre-ft, Tucson stub out gray water of 32,570 acre-ft, and Tucson`s reclaimed wastewater of 15,750 acre-ft. for a total of 98,777 acre-ft. In addition, the following water losses need calculation: swamp cooler evaporation, city-3 farm irrigation, building misting systems, swimming and Jacuzzi evaporation, construction water, septic tank losses, recharge pond evaporation, biosolid moisture content, and other losses to be discovered.

An annual detailed total water input analysis minus the total annual detailed water losses results in the quantity of water remaining for annual sustainability of the existent population, government use, commercial use, industrial use, and, if excess water is available, growth. City altering of allocations and priorities can be revised for mandated or desired changes to the input parameters. Costs and potable water are two subsets of data which contribute to the total water use acceptable to the elected city council and citizens of Tucson.

subsequent action would be at the discretion of the responsible and accountable

elected officials.

An alternative is a contract for Sustainability and Water Management with Kathy

Jacobs, Director, of the intra university Arizona Water Institute.

Respectfully, Clyde H. Stagner, a citizen of Tucson and Pima County

---

cstampingr@dakotacom.net

From: "cstampingr@dakotacom.net" <cstamping@dakotacom.net>
To: <info@tucsonpimawaterstudy.com>
Sent: Wednesday, September 10, 2008 11:47 AM
Subject: Re: Meeting Notice Oct 2008-Sustainability-written comment

Water Sustainability within the Tucson Water Bottle
Sustainable Water=Water Input-Water Flow(export)-Water Evaporation(export)

Apply Adaptive Management to the listed parameters for access and retention of water within the Tucson Water Bottle. Annual and future annual analysis.

WATER INPUT	WATER EVAPORATION
Tucson Basin Natural Recharge	Swamp Coolers
Avra Valley Natural Recharge	Park/ Golf course Irrigation
CAP Allocation	City-3farm CAP Irrigation
Havested Rainwater to Sewer	Govt. Facility Irrigation
Air Water Generators*	Bldg. Misting Systems
Reclaimed Influent Recharge**	Residence Graywater Irrigation
Bottled Water/Drinks Imported	Rainwater Harvesting Irrigation
Other Actual water Input	Fire Fighting
Purchased/Indian Nation	Car Washing
Purchased Groundwater	Water Dept Leaks/Losses
	Swimming Pools
*Infinite sustainable supply of water	Ponds/lakes
**Potable or Nonpotable	Manufacturing Processes
	Construction Water
WATER FLOW(EXPORT)	Residence Irrigation
Biosolids Moisture Export	Septic Tank Receipts
Bottled Water/Drink Export	Other
Santa Cruz River WW Discharge	

WATER(for prioritizing&allocation)
Potable Drinking Water,Residential***
Potable Drinking Water,Nonresidential***
Reclaimed Effluent,Residential
Reclaimed Effluent,Nonresidential
Effluent to Recharge
Residential Growth
Nonresidential Growth

***Obtain Tucson Water Dept.`s definitions:prioritizing and allocating requires definitive delineation and differential itemizing.
Note:Detailed applicable data for each entity recorded into a database for computer access using software which relates the Adaptive Management variables would enhance this analysis and evaluation for solutions.
A Tucson citizens methodology and protocol,Clyde H. Stagner-10 Sept 08

From: "cstampingr@dakotacom.net" <cstamping@dakotacom.net>
To: <info@tucsonpimawaterstudy.com>
Sent: Saturday, August 23, 2008 2:56 PM
Subject: Fw: After quality,quantity sustainability

Info-clyde
----- Original Message -----
From: cstampingr@dakotacom.net
To: mcweb@tucsonaz.gov
Sent: Saturday, August 23, 2008 2:51 PM
Subject: After quality,quantity sustainability

Dear Mayor and Council Members,
   Since state agencies are involved,this request is sent to the Mayor and Council instead of the applicable city entity.
   Under the provisions of Permit No. 71-564896.0001,CAP is required to estimate the daily evaporation (Ref:Permit Conditions;4,Monitoring Requirements;d,Operational Monitoring Requirements,ii-) from the wetted areas,in acres, within the Avra Valley Recharge Project for recharge basins:RB-1,RB-2,RB-3,and RB-4. Is this evaporative loss of water from these recharge basins debited to Tucson`s annual 144,000 Cap water allocation? If so,what was the total annual 2007 CAP reduction in acre-feet?
   For all Tucson Water Dept. supplied open water recharge basins/open water storage areas/recreational ponds,lakes/other ,what is the total water evaporation in acre-feet from their wetted surfaces, individually identified, as specified in,"Evaporation from Open Water Surfaces ,in Arizona, by Keiyh R. Cooley,1970 (Ref:Permit No. 71-564896.0001, cited supra.
   From swimming pool surface areas determined from Pima County Health Dept. swimming pool permits, what is their annual loss of potable water,in acre feet, due to evaporation.
   What was the 2007 annual total wastewater effluent,in acre-feet, supplied to Commercial,Industrial,Government,and others.For each of the above identities,what was the total estimated evaporative loss in annul acre-feet? If the total acre-feet supplied does not equal the total evaporative loss, what was the disposition of the difference in quantities?
   This information is essential for water sustainability debits and credits.
   Respectfully,Clyde H. Stagner,a Tucson citizen

From:	"cstampingr@dakotacom.net" <cstamping@dakotacom.net>
To:	"Jeff Prevatt" <Jeff.Prevatt@wwm.pima.gov>
Cc:	"Ward2 Ward2" <Ward2@tucsonaz.gov>
Sent:	Monday, April 07, 2008 6:10 PM
Subject:	Re: Testing

Jeff,

Thank you for responding. As a citizen of Tucson,recent news articles and phases of planning for tucson`s water future indicate consideration for converting sewage effluent into potable water. To date the publicity priming has had a priority of quantity.Coliform testing is used to indicate whether potentially harmful bacteria may be present.

This citizen proposes a first planning prioity of determining a baseline for possible contaminants of all detrimental virsuses and pathogens(other than bacteria) cited in the Clean Water Act,as amended,which have an MCL of zero.Your attention is invited to Chapter 1 of the USEPA MANUALOF METHODS FOR VIROLOGY.EPA/600/4-84/013 for testing parameters and methodology.

In addition,suggest liaison with the University of Arizona and US Public Health Service for determination of possible pharmaceuticals testing of effluent(Ref:WCP Online:Pharmceuticals in Drinking Water Supplies).

In the early 1960`s an engineering manual stated that chlorine was unacceptable for killing virus. Aborting ultraviolet disinfection for chlorine is interesting should the chlorine be a linear disinfectant rather than exponential.

Priority one test results could be supportive,or detrimental, to Tucson growth.Since you are a member of the organization being tested, bonding of your personnel may be appropriate- should your office do the testing suggested in priority one.

The comments herein are offered in support of making Tucson the greatest place to live-there is no intention of finding fault.

The best-clyde

---

cstampingr@dakotacom.net

From:	"cstampingr@dakotacom.net" <cstamping@dakotacom.net>
To:	"John Kmiec" <John.Kmiec@tucsonaz.gov>
Sent:	Wednesday, May 14, 2008 10:25 AM
Subject:	Re: NOVA Referral: Open//Water (Other) 31142-33135

Dear Mr.Kmiec.

Your response is informative but without scientific evidence that drinking water monitoring samples not taken,or subsequently lost after taken, would contained,or contained less than the health-based contaminant level.

These concerns and doubts about the sustainable quality of Tucson`s drinking water can be negated by the Tucson Water System becoming a part of this nation`s 76 % of drinking water systems which have no reporting/monitoring violations.

As a Tucson citizen and taxpayer, I solicit your resonse as to the cause for the Tucson Water System having the 63 USEPA previously cited water monitoring violations and the solution for elimination of future monitoring violations as 76 % of this nation`s drinking water system have done.

No content of this message is intended to adversely criticize you,Mr Kmiec,or any of your employees.

Appreciatively and respectfully-clyde h stagner Original Message -----
From: "John Kmiec" <   >
To: <   >
Cc: "Christopher Avery" <   >; "Jeff Biggs"
<   >; "Mitch Basefsky" <   >;
<   >
Sent: Wednesday, May 14, 2008 9:14 AM
Subject: NOVA Referral: Open//Water (Other) 31142-33135

From: "cstampingr@dakotacom.net" <cstamping@dakotacom.net>
To: <info@tucsonpimawaterstudy.com>
Sent: Saturday, August 23, 2008 10:53 AM
Subject: Fw: TW Webmail

Dear Sirs,
  Research of documents yielded zero results- quantification of water supplied was prolifically related to individual and residential water usage.. This data is necessary for inclusion in computations for annual credits and debits n a sustainability analysis-clyde
---- Original Message -----
From: cstampingr@dakotacom.net
To: TW_Web1@tucsonaz.gov
Cc: TW_Web6@tucsonaz.gov
Sent: Saturday, August 23, 2008 10:39 AM
Subject: TW Webmail

Dear Sirs;
  What was the 2007 annual total water, in gallons, supplied by Tucson Water Dept, to each of the following:
  Commercial (Potable Water)   _____
  Commercial (WasteWater Effluent)_____
  Industrial (Potable Water)   _____
  Industrial (WasteWater Effluent)   _____
  Gov`t(Potable Water)   _____
  Gov`t(WasteWater Effluent)   _____
  Other(Potable Water)   _____
  Other(WasteWater Effluent)   _____
Sincerely,Clyde H Stagner

From: "cstampingr@dakotacom.net" <cstamping@dakotacom.net>
To: <mcweb@tucsonaz.gov>
Sent: Saturday, September 27, 2008 10:43 AM
Subject: Politics vs Water

Dear Honorable Mayor and Tucson Councilpersons,
  The increase in population between 2008 and 2030 is estimated to be 655,799. With an average size family of three persons, the increase in households is 218,600. The $500.00 per residence for stub-out plumbing represents $109,300,000 in additional monetary input into Tucson for vendors,plumbers,and tax receipts. Should all residences install $5,0000.00 graywater systems, an additional input of $1,093,000,000 would flow into the Tucson economy during the period 2010-2030.
  For this same period, Mr Tannler, Director ADWC,Tucson TAMA, has been apprised that the TAMA water budget`s annual riparian (evapotranspiration) water budget loss of 3,700 acre-ft annually could increase by 28,890 acre-ft annually due to residential graywater riparian(evapotranspiration) water loss. The potential residential graywater loss is equal to 20.06 % of Tucson`s annual allocation of CAP surface water.
  During the past several months, email correspondence has been received from Mr. Jeff B. Biggs, newly appointed Director of the Tucson Water Dept.. In every message, Mr. Biggs has been forthright, helpful, and responsive with conclusive remark offering help with any additional problem or comment offered. Mr. Biggs gives facts without equivocation. His assistance was, and is, thankfully appreciated.
  My gratitude to the Mayor ,Tucson Councilpersons, and the Tucson governmental protocol for allowing,considering, and responding to a citizen`s viewpoints,scientific input, and concerns over the past severa months.
  Respectfully, Clyde H Stagner, a Tucson citizen.

Tucson Pima Water Study Members,   24 Sept. 2008
Dear Members,   Subject: Organization of Sustainability

TAMA` s "Safe Yield" can be interpreted as TAMA` sustainability. The complexity

of variables necessitates Adaptive Management for quantity, quality, and cost if

Applicable. For example, the TAMA budget cites an annual evapotranspiration of

3,700 acre ft annually through 2025, mainly in the Upper Santa Cruz. However, the

Tucson plumbing code, promulgated on 23 Sept. 2008, can cause an annual loss of

32,570 acre ft of gray water evapotranspiration (Ref:TAMA/Tucson

Evapotranspiration, Clyde H. Stagner, to Tucson Pima Water Study Members, 24

Sept. 2008).

 Quantity(monitoring),Quality(monitoring), and cost(for prioritizing and

allocation) data are necessary to keep the Sustainability Adaptive Management

system viable for evaluations. These variables require user identification for

applicability. Tucson Water Dept.` s designation of only two users, Nonresidential

and Total Deliveries(Ref: Tom Arnold,Tucso Water, email) is inadequate for

sustainability Adaptive Management. An example of required input data is (Ref:

Pima County Effluent Generation and Utilization Report, 2004) annual acre ft

effluent from the Metropolitan Treatment Facility for Calendar Year 2004for:

Arthur Pack Golf Course	581.4
Silverbell Golf Course	533.5
Kino Sports Complex*	329.92

  *at cost of $189,281.17 for an acre ft cost of $573.72

Additional data is available in the above cited reference. Note that similar data is

required from the Tucson Water Dept.

To obtain monitoring data from the Pima Waste Water Management, a records request is required (Ref:Jeff Prevat,PimaWWM,email). To view Avra Valley ground water and surface CAP monitoring data reqires a physical presence at TAMA Hq. on Congress St. All quality, quantity, and costs applicable to water sustainability requires a comprehensive, exclusive mandate for openess and availability to the public and governmental entities-preferably in a centralized data bank.

Mr. Jeff Tannier, Director ADWR, Tucson AMA, has described TAMA`s Water Budget for Safe Yield and sustainability. Today, Sustainable Endowments Institute, Rockefeller Philanthropy Advisors released their 2009 Report Card for 200 colleges and universities. The College Sustainability Report Card gave Arizona State a B+. Stanford University received an A+ and 14th ranking. The Director, Sustainability and Energy Management, Joseph Stagner(my son), was dubbed a Sustainability Czar by the university newspaper(Ref: newspaper article).

What is the legacy of the Tucson Pima Water Study Oversight Committee? The Committees present purview includes paradox autoanalysis, politically sensitive independents situated in turf guarding governmental pay and positions- which is their sustainability. A Tucson/Pima Czar for Sustainability and Water Management with authoritative accountability,responsibility,and cost analysis is Indicated . The Czar and his staff should be independent of Tucson and/or Pima County` s Managers and report to joint official sessions of the Tucson Council and Pima County Supervisors in the presence of the Managers. Implementation and

CONCLUSION

Tucson Water Department water monitoring violations, lack of annual water quality baseline concentrations for Clearwater blend and reclaimed effluent sediments, radon, radioactive potassium, pharmaceuticals, perchlorate, and endocrine disrupters indicates the need for a Tucson Water Quality Department, or preferably, a Tucson/Pima Municipal Water Quality Laboratory for assessing mandatory or human health monitoring needs; conducting potable water, biosolids, and effluent monitoring; conducting laboratory analyses; and posting timely data results on the internet without equivocation.

The elected City Council of Tucson has yet to act upon the

1. Tucson Water Department`s citation for the need of a TDS numerical concentration for TDS by 2006.

2. Group 3, Tucsom Basin Desalinization Project`s recommendations for desalinization.

3. Clean Colorado Rivers Coalition, appointed by the Governor, concern for seven pollutants, considered by experts, requiring continued assessment.

4. U.S. Bureau of Reclamation and Tucson Water Departments`s recommendations for desalinization of Tucson`s CAP surface water allocation.

5. USEPA water monitoring violations by the Tucson Water Department.

6. Pima County`s commitment to cessation of additional golf courses.

7. Presence of effluent in the Clearwater potable blend. Tucson User`s Bill of Rights, Section 14 (c) (1), states, "No effluent shall ever be added to, or blended with, the drinking water supply. Note: Las Vegas effluent is discharged into Lake Mead. Perchlorate enters the Las Vegas Wash and then enters Lake Mead. Perchlorates were detected and measured in the CAVSARP and Avra Valley recharge wells in 2004 by ADEQ who also measured perchlorates in the Santa Cruz River Pima wastewater effluent in 2004. The Tucson Water Dept detected and measured perchorates in Tucson`s potable water in 2001. CAP measured per chlorates in CAP surface water at the San Xavier Pumping station in 2006. Perchlorate was measured in six samples of untreated CAP water at the Clearwater site between October 1997 -April 2000. Perchlorates have tagged Las Vegas effluent to Tucson`s potable water.

Infinite sustainability is unattainable. Increased population growth for Tucson requires population boundary limitations or the conversion of wastewater effluent to potable drinking water as Orange County ,California, has done.

www.ingramcontent.com/pod-product-compliance
Lightning Source LLC
Chambersburg PA
CBHW052003280526

45793CB00005B/836